Fir[illegible] in Chess

CADOGAN CHESS SERIES

Other titles for the novice player include:

LEV ALBURT
Test and Improve Your Chess

YURI AVERBAKH
Chess Endings: Essential Knowledge

JOSÉ CAPABLANCA
Chess Fundamentals

JULIAN HODGSON
Chess Travellers Quiz Book

DANIEL KING
How Good is Your Chess?

DANIEL KOPEC et al
Mastering Chess

STEWART REUBEN
Chess Openings – Your Choice

VLADIMIR VUKOVIC
The Art of Attack in Chess

JOHN WALKER
Chess for Tomorrow's Champions

JOHN WALKER
Chess Openings for Juniors

JOHN WALKER
Test Your Chess: Piece Power

SIMON WEBB
Chess for Tigers

BARUCH WOOD
Easy Guide to Chess

First Steps in Chess

J.N. Walker

Illustrated by Paul Hambridge

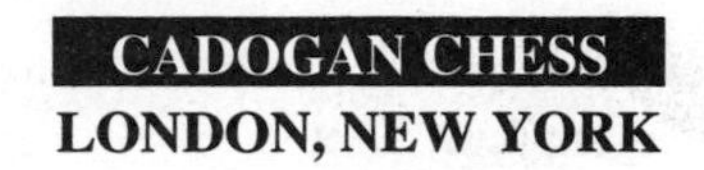

CADOGAN BOOKS DISTRIBUTION

UK/EUROPE/AUSTRALASIA/ASIA/AFRICA
Distribution: Grantham Book Services Ltd, Isaac Newton Way,
Alma Park Industrial Estate, Grantham, Lincs NG31 9SD.
Tel: (01476) 67421; Fax: (01476) 590223.

USA/CANADA/LATIN AMERICA/JAPAN
Distribution: Paramount Distribution Center, Front & Brown Streets,
Riverside, New Jersey 08075, USA.
Tel: (609) 461 6500; Fax: (609) 764 9122.

First published 1978 by Oxford University Press.

This edition published 1995 by Cadogan Books plc, London House,
Parkgate Road, London SW11 4NQ.

Offset from the Oxford University Press edition of First Steps in Chess.
Reprinted by kind permission of Oxford University Press.

British Library Cataloguing in Publication Data
A CIP catalogue record for this book is available from the British Library.

ISBN 1 85744 190 7

Cover design by Artisan Design Factory, High Wycombe.
Printed in Great Britain by BPC Wheatons Ltd, Exeter.

Contents

Acknowledgements

This book was the brain-child of Adam Hart-Davis. Adam came up with a whole string of ideas about content, style and layout before the writing even got under way – he then emigrated halfway through page one leaving me to do all the work! I tracked him down to his hide-out north of Huddersfield, however, and there was no escape a second time. Thanks Adam; without your excellent – 'brilliant', I think you prefer to call it – help and advice, this book would never have been written.

The teaching method has been tested for several years by a great number of children, and modifications have been made in the light of their experience. My thanks go to them all but especially to Paul Perrett and Martin Goodey for their comments at the time of writing.

The 250 diagrams were prepared by William Gardner. My thanks to him also for undertaking the enormous task of checking and rechecking the proofs with such care and precision and for appearing in person with one of his many friends on page 63.

The splendid pictures are the work of Paul Hambridge. When you are only twelve the prospect of drawing pictures to illustrate a book is an exciting challenge. Drawing can be fun but when you are working for an exacting task-master who demands perfection, it can be a test of character where patience and determination are as important as artistic ability. Well done Hammy!

Introduction

Chess is a very old game. Nobody knows when it was first played. What we do know is that people in ancient India played a game of war with pieces on a board; that this game spread to Persia, that the Arabs conquered Persia and later brought the game to Europe. Because the game was passed on from country to country, over hundreds of years, its rules obviously changed a lot. The original Indian game was called chaturanga, and it got this name from the four sections of the Indian army. The pieces represented the king and his adviser together with the four fighting units: horses, chariots, elephants, and infantry. The Indian army stopped using chariots around 326 B.C. when they proved useless against Alexander the Great's invading forces; so this gives us a good idea that the first form of chess must have been played over 2500 years ago!

In this book you will learn to play chess step by step. You will begin knowing nothing. At the first step you will learn about the board, later steps will tell you about the pieces, and the final steps will help you to improve and win your games. After some of the steps you will be given a small game to play using just a few of the pieces. This is a new way of learning the game; it will help you to fix the rules and the moves of the pieces firmly in your mind. You can if you wish move straight on from step to step ignoring these little games. But try to be patient; this new way of learning has been tested, and it works! If you follow the instructions you will still quickly learn all about the game, and you will find chess easy to play because you will *understand* what you are doing.

Then you will win!

The Battlefield

Chess is not just a game.
Chess is a battle.
A battle from days gone by when great armies met.
Soldiers with pikes and swords, archers, cavalry, and cannon to blast away at the enemy lines.
The two sides gathered their men and faced each other across the field.
The men waited anxiously.
Uniforms, red and gold, shone proudly in all their glory.
Armour glinted in the sunlight.
Banners, unfurled, fluttered in the breeze.
The moment for battle drew near.
The generals made their final plans.
The time had come.
The first shots were fired.
Cannons rumbled and filled the air with smoke, flame, and ball.
Muskets crackled, arrows flashed, cavalry charged, and the infantry advanced, screaming their bloodthirsty warcries.

In chess there are no soldiers with pikes and swords.
There are no archers, no cavalry, and no cannon to blast away at the enemy lines.
There are only thirty-two chess-men; sixteen white, and sixteen black.
They are not alive; they are not real.
But they can fight!
They can fight just like real soldiers and real weapons.
Each different chess-man has its own way of moving, its own way of fighting.
All the pieces need is a field upon which to fight.
The chess-board with its sixty-four squares is their battlefield.

You are going to be a general!
You are going to take charge of one of the chess armies.
Your opponent will command the other army.
You will have to make plans for attack and defence.
You must make your army fight well.

You have probably heard those splendid stories about how the general gallantly charged into battle at the head of his army. How, fearing no danger, he spurred his horse on and single-handed cut half the enemy army to pieces. How his bravery and strength set a shining example to the rest of his men.

Well, it didn't really happen like that!
Or, at least, not very often.
The soldier who led the charge at the enemy lines was the soldier most likely to get shot!
A dead general is not much use.

No, the general sat up on top of a hill, right out of harm's way. He sat where he could watch the whole battlefield, or as much of it as possible, where he could make his plans in safety, where he could see clearly how the battle was going.

You must do just the same at the chess-board.
Sit behind your army; don't peer at the board from the side; don't lounge lazily.
Sit up straight so you can see the board clearly; then, like the general, you will be able to plan your battle properly.

The first thing you must remember to do is to get your battlefield the right way round.

☐ **Each player must have a white square in the right-hand corner of the chess-board nearest to him.**

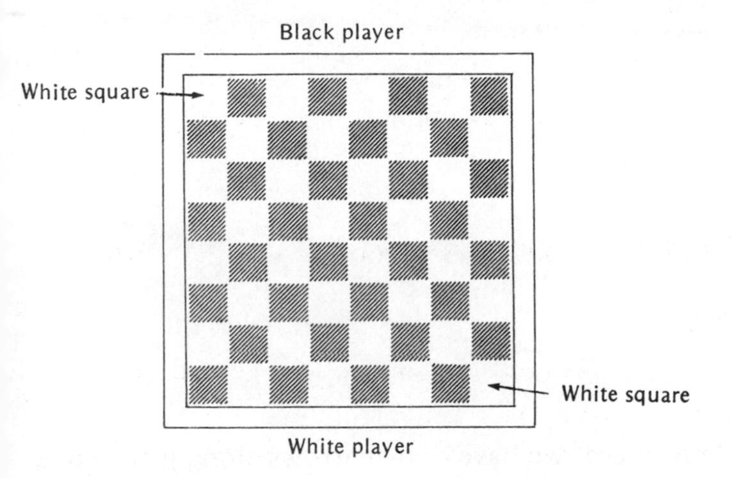

Remember the rhyme, and it's easy: **White on the right.**

The two halves of the chess-board are called the King's side and the Queen's side.
The half to White's right is the King's side.
The half to White's left is the Queen's side.

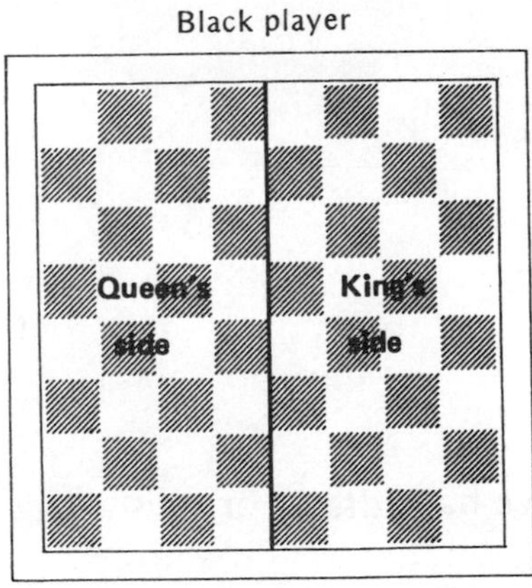

Now you have the board the right way round, let us have a good look at our battlefield.
We will give names to different parts of the board.

A row of squares running from one player to the other is called a **file**.

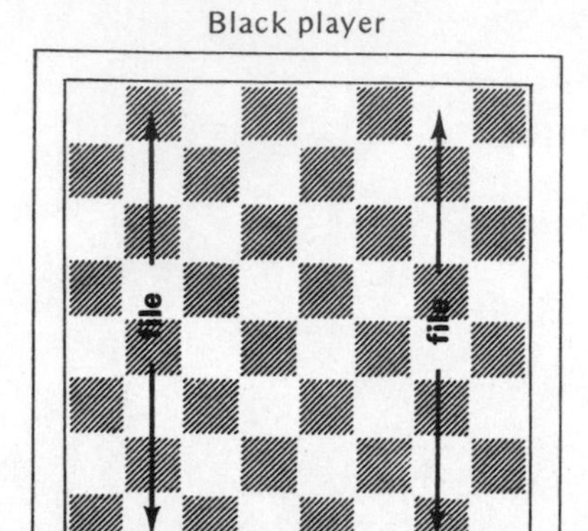

There are eight files on a chess-board; we have drawn arrows along just two of them.

A row of squares running across the board from side to side is called a **rank**.

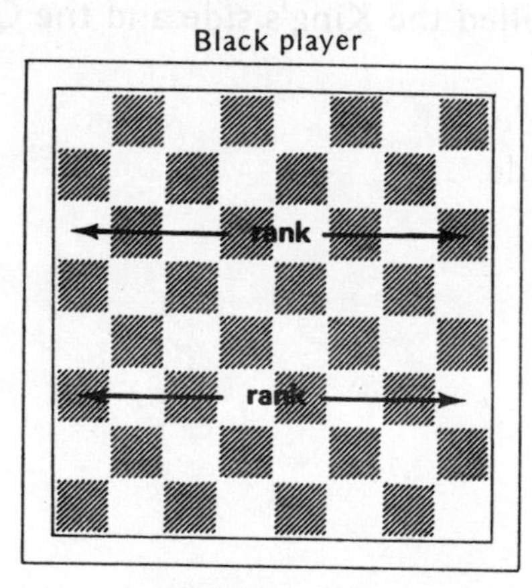

There are eight ranks on a chess-board; we have drawn arrows along just two of them.

A row of squares of the same colour slanting across the board is called a **diagonal**.

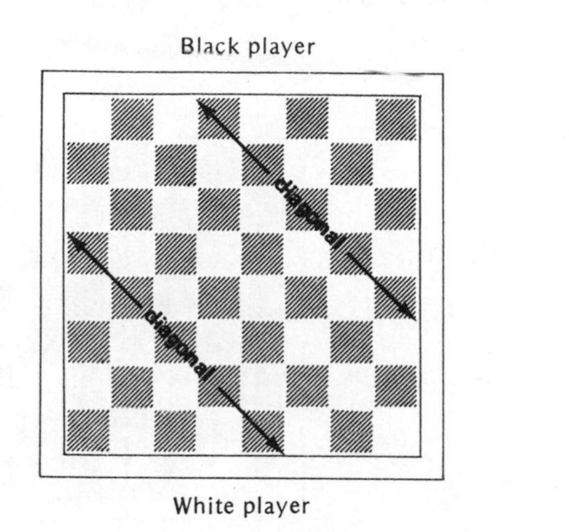

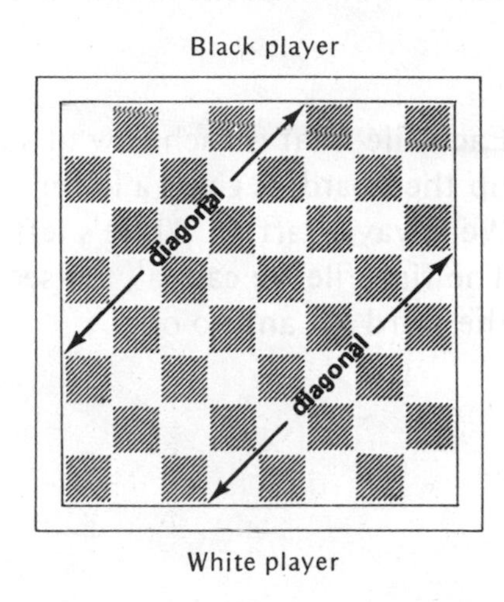

There are many diagonals on a chess-board. Some are white, some are black; some slant to the right, some to the left. In our two diagrams we have drawn arrows along just four of them.

The four squares in the middle of the board we call the **centre**.

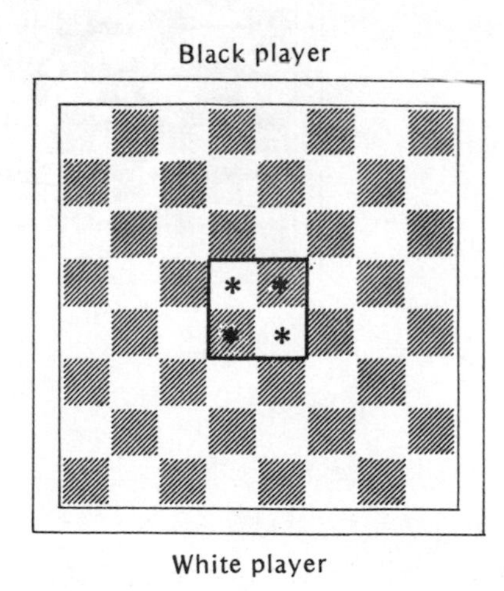

We have marked each of the four centre squares with a star.

Naming Squares

We are going to give a name to each of the 64 squares; this will help us to talk about different moves later on in the book.

Each file, that is each row of squares running up the board, is given a letter.
We always start on White's left.
The first file we call 'a', the second file 'b', the third 'c', and so on.

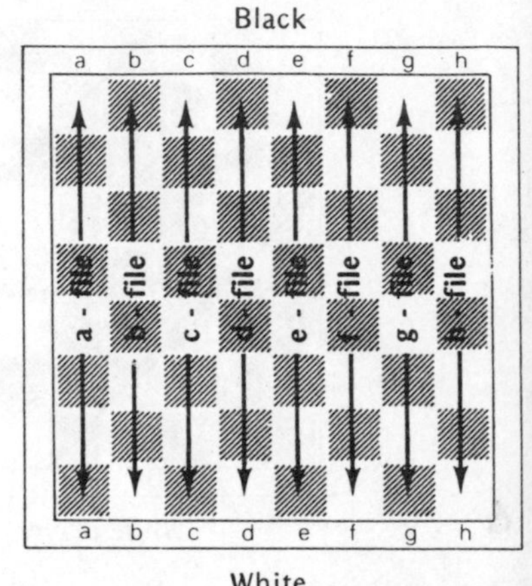

Each rank, that is each row of squares running across the board, has a number.
We always start at White's end.
The first rank we call '1', the second rank '2', the third '3', and so on.

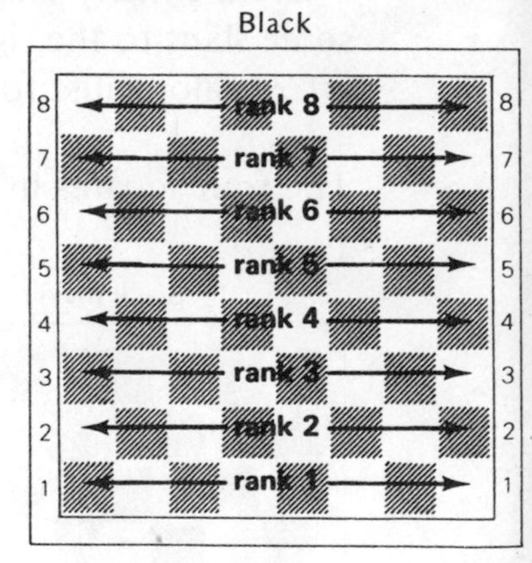

Now that every file and every rank has a name, we can name each of the squares.

Look at the black circle in the diagram.
It is in file ‘c’.
It is in rank ‘3’.
So the square with the black circle is called ‘c3’.

Look now at the white circle.
It is in file ‘g’ and rank ‘6’; so the square with the white circle is called ‘g6’.

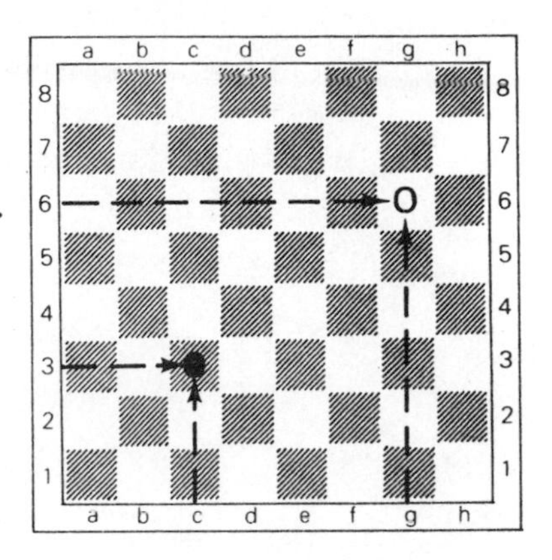

All the squares get their names the same way.

Remember!
First the file letter.
Then the rank number.

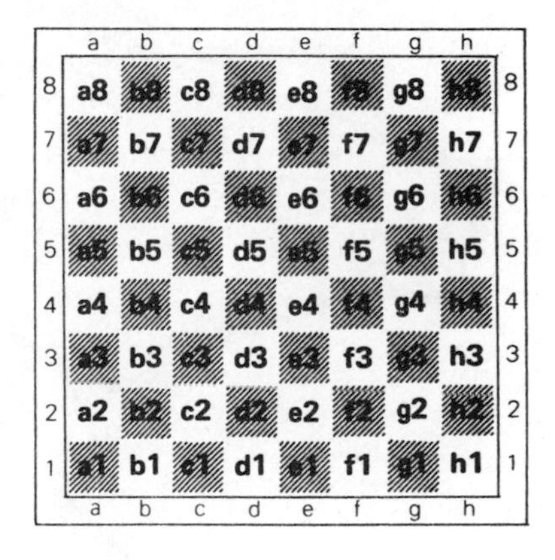

The Pawn

The ordinary foot-soldier in the Indian army was called a 'poon'. In our language the word 'poon' has changed to 'pawn', and so the pawn is the foot-soldier of our chess army. As you might have guessed, the pawn has the lowest value of all the chess pieces.

- ☐ **Each player has eight pawns.**
- ☐ **The pawns begin the game lined up as a row of sentries on the second rank in front of each player.**

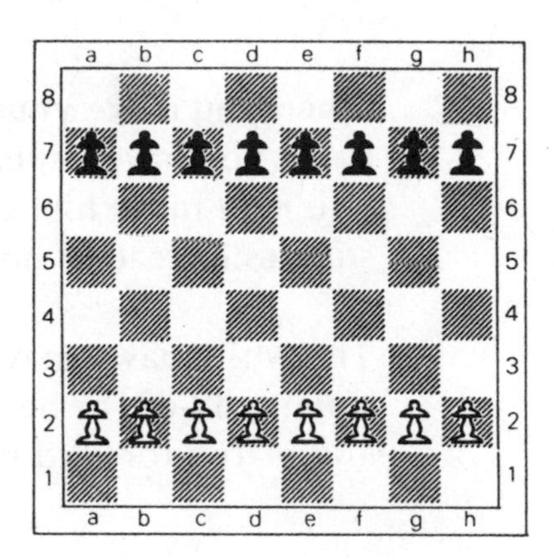

- ☐ **The normal move for the pawn is to march straight foward one square.**

In the diagram the white pawn may move forward one square, from c3 to c4.
(We write this move down as **c3-c4**.)

The black pawn may also move straight forward one square, from f5 to f4.
(This we write **. . . f5-f4**.)

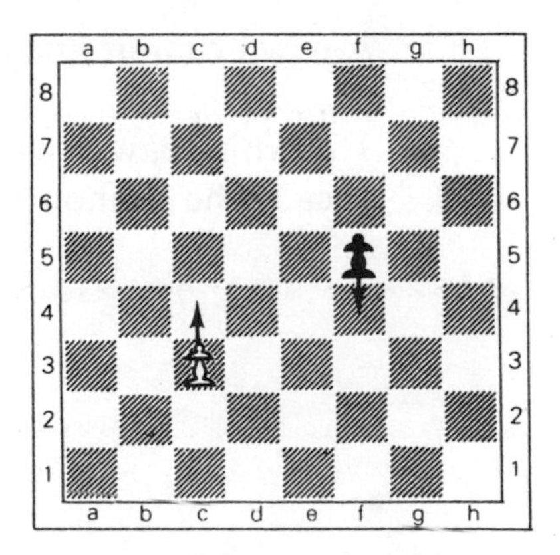

☐ **A pawn cannot move straight forward to a square already occupied.**

The white pawn cannot move forward from e4 to e5 because a black pawn is already standing on that square.

For the same reason the black pawn cannot move forward from e5 to e4.

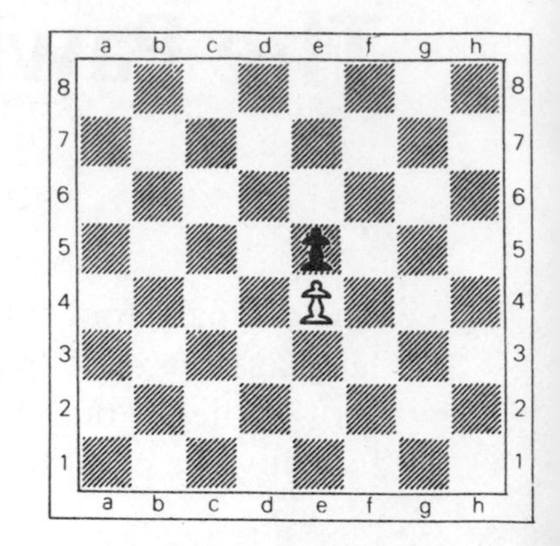

☐ **When you make your first move with each pawn you have a special choice; if you like you may move him straight forward two squares instead of one.**

The white pawn may move forward one square, **d2-d3**, or he can use his special move and march forward two squares, **d2-d4**.

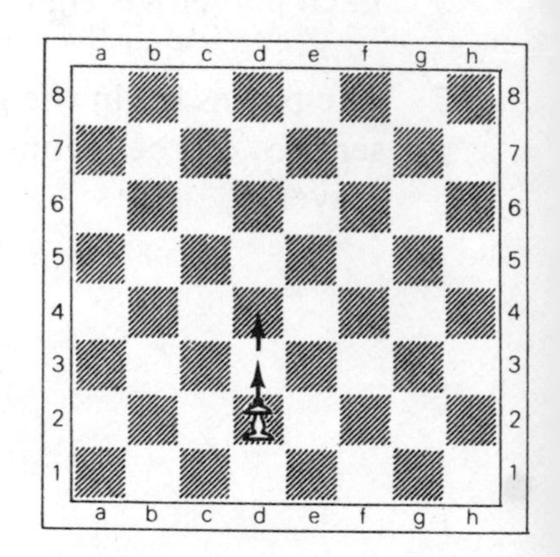

☐ **A pawn cannot jump.**

The white pawn cannot move from d2 to d4, because he cannot jump over the black pawn on d3.

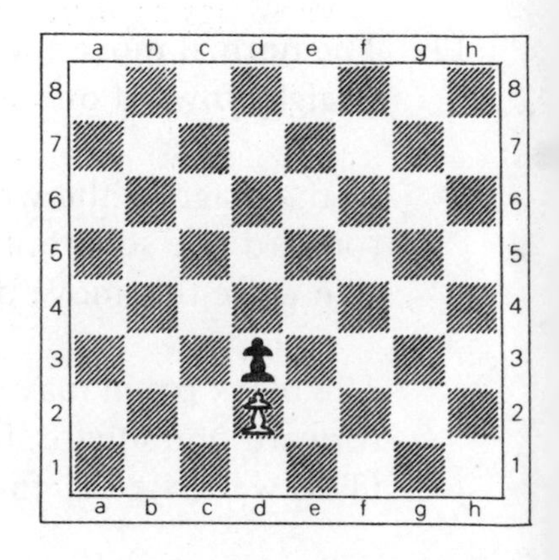

☐ **A pawn captures by moving one square diagonally forward.**

The white pawn attacks two squares, b5 and d5.

The black pawn attacks two squares, d6 and f6.

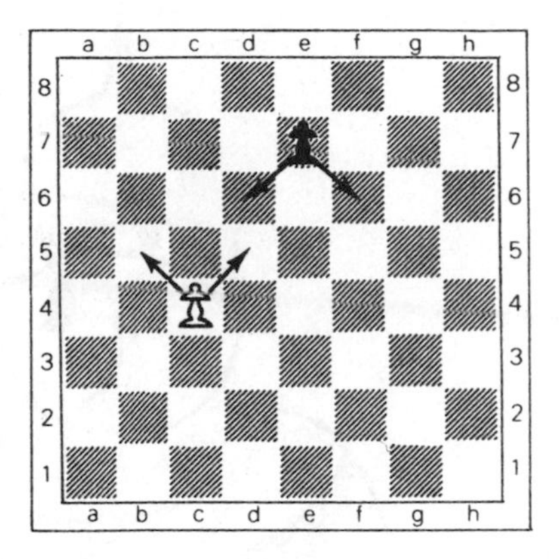

The white pawn on e4 and the black pawn on d5 are attacking each other.

It is White's turn to move; if he wants to, he may capture the black pawn.

White does not have to capture, but he may do so if he wishes.

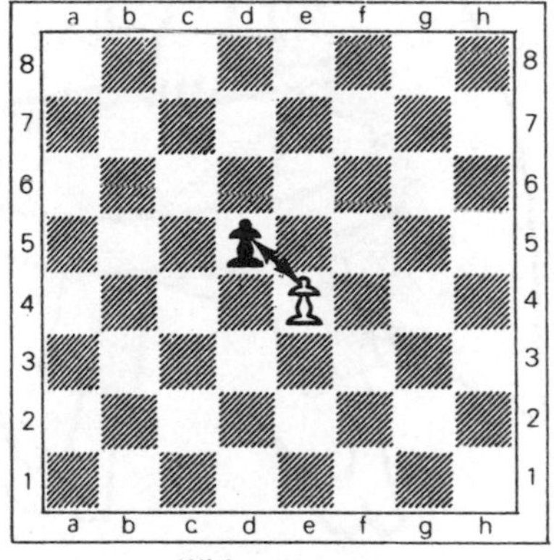

White to move

White has captured the black pawn.

White has taken the black pawn off the board, and his own pawn has moved diagonally forward one square.

Since the white pawn on e4 has captured the black pawn on d5 we write this move **e4xd5**.

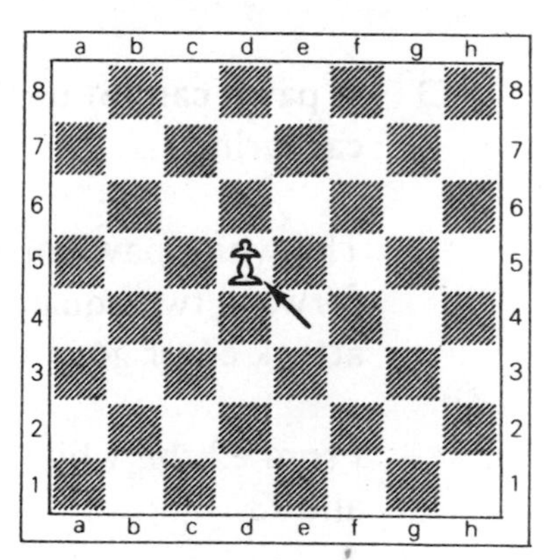

Position after e4xd5

□ **A pawn cannot use its special first move for capturing.**

The white pawn on e2 can move straight forward two squares to e4, but it does not attack c4 or g4.

From e2 the white pawn only attacks d3 and f3.

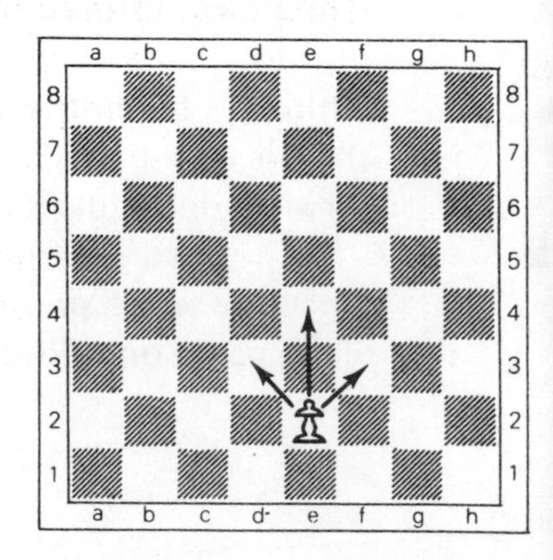

Before we go any further, we will test what you have learnt.
Look at the diagram below.
You are White; how many different moves can you make?

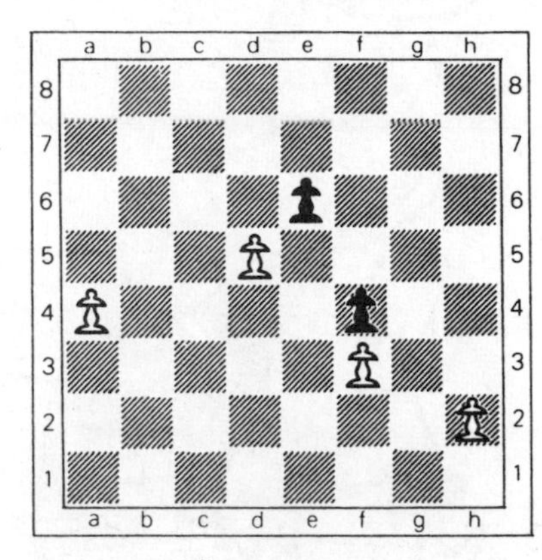

White to move

Did you find all of White's possible moves?
You should have found five.
Let's look at each pawn in turn and see what they are:

The pawn on a4 has only one move:

He can march straight forward one square to a5.

The pawn on d5 has two moves:

He can move forward one square to d6.
He can capture the black pawn on e6.

The pawn on f3 cannot move:

There are no black pawns for him to capture, and he cannot march forward because he is blocked by the black pawn on f4.

The pawn on h2 has two moves:

He can move forward one square to h3.
He can use his special first move and march forward two squares to h4.

So altogether White has five possible moves: **a4-a5, d5-d6, d5xe6, h2-h3,** and **h2-h4**.

Pawns

Set up your board with the pawns in their starting positions, just like the diagram.

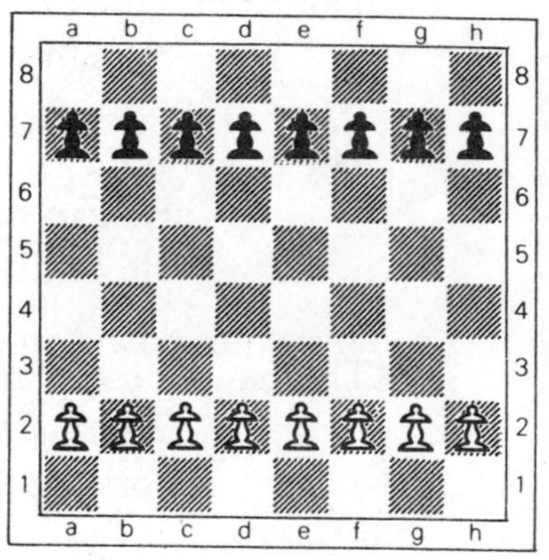

The game of Pawns

Now you are ready for your first game. This is a game called 'Pawns', which will help you get used to the way the pawn moves, and make it much easier for you to play real chess.

The rules are simple:
The two players move in turn, with White having first go.
The two players move and capture in the way we have already explained.
The winner is the first person to get one of his pawns to the other end of the board.

White begins. He picks up his pawn on e2 and moves it straight forward two squares to e4. Now it is Black's turn. He picks up his pawn on g7 and moves it forward just one square to g6.
Your board should now look like the diagram on the right.
We will write the moves in chess language:

1 e2-e4 g7-g6

Can you see what we have done?
We have first of all written the move number '1'; then we have written White's move on the left and Black's move on the right.

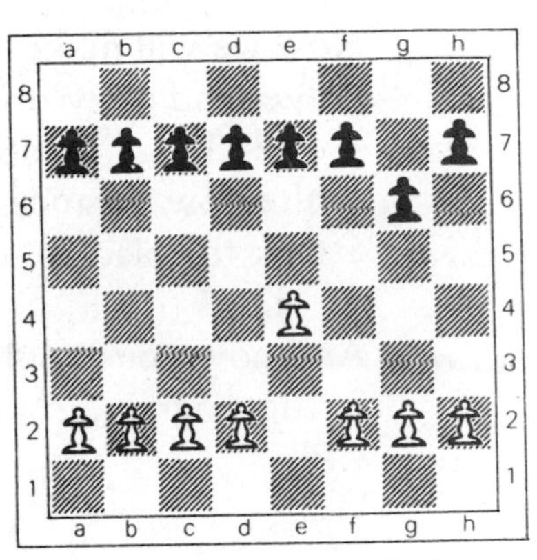

Position after 1 . . . g7-g6

Now we'll carry on with the game and make the second move for each player:

2 d2-d4 f7-f5

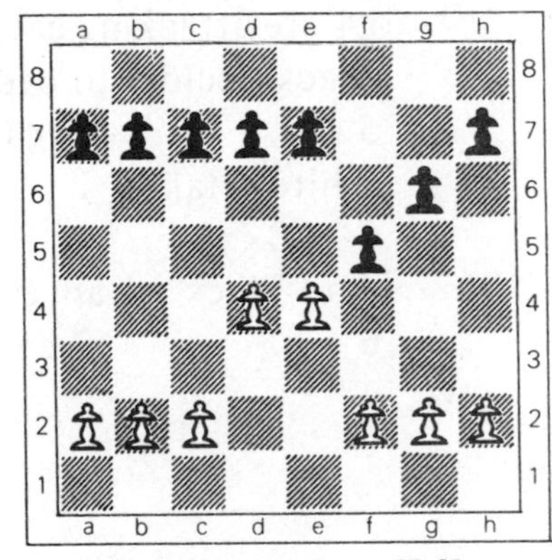

Position after 2 . . . f7-f5

The white pawn on e4 is attacking the black pawn on f5. White captures:

3 e4xf5

Black takes back:

3 . . . g6xf5

Now after three moves your board should look like the diagram on the right.

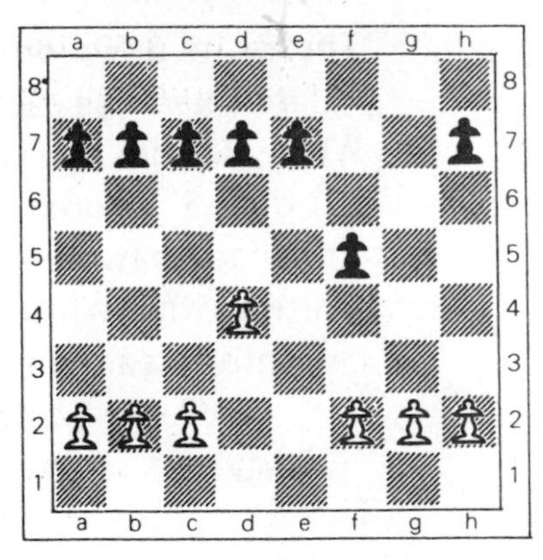

Position after 3 . . . g6xf5

Now we will make the fourth moves for each player and carry on with the game.

4 f2-f3 d7-d6

White now advances his pawn from g2 to attack the black pawn on f5:

5 g2-g4

And now you should have reached the position in the diagram.

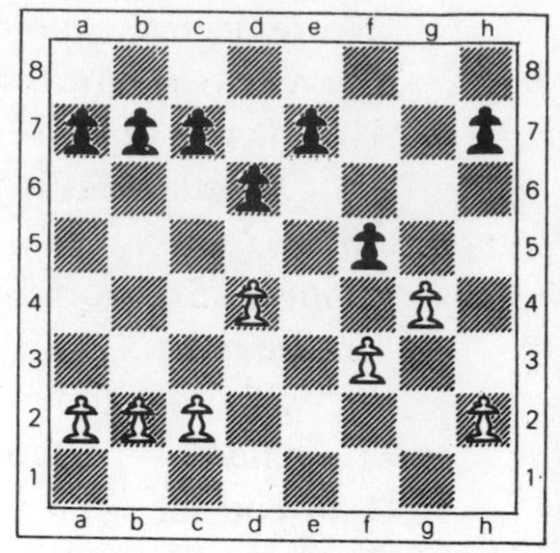

Position after 5 g2-g4

The black pawn on f5 and the white pawn on g4 are attacking each other.

Black decides to capture.

5 ... f5xg4

White retakes.

6 f3xg4

And Black advances a pawn in the middle.

6 ... e7-e5

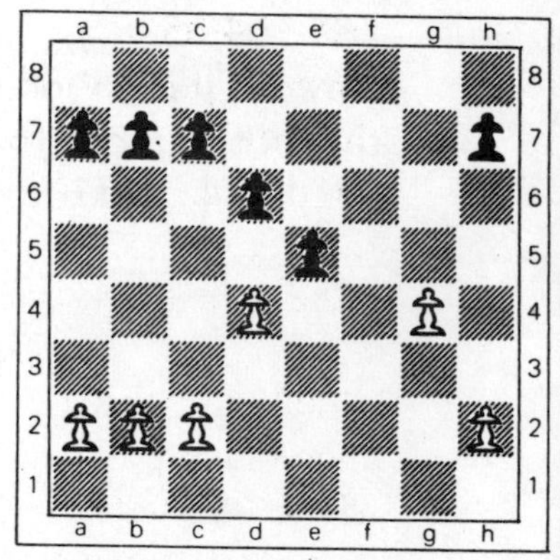

Position after 6 ... e7-e5

The white pawn on d4 and the black pawn on e5 are attacking each other.

White decides to exchange pawns.

7 d4xe5 d6xe5

The black pawn on e5 is now clear of all the white pawns. White cannot stop it from marching steadily forward to e1.

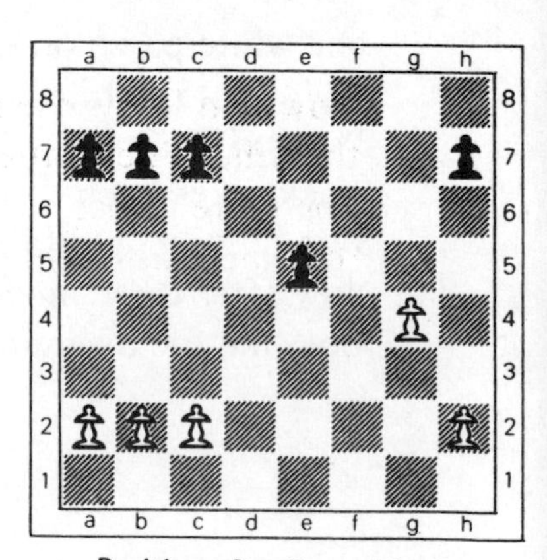

Position after 7 ... d6xe5

As he cannot stop Black's pawn from reaching home, White tries hard to race through one of his own pawns.

8 h2-h4 e5-e4

The black pawn marches happily on . . .

9 g4-g5 e4-e3

. . . and on.

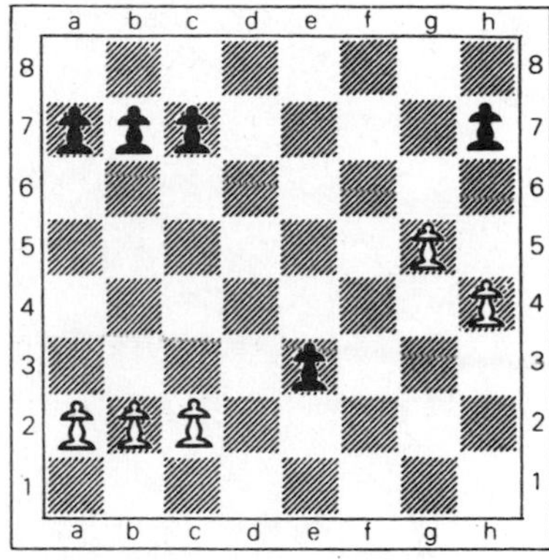

Position after 9 . . . e4-e3

10 h4-h5

White's pawns also march forward, but Black is winning the race.

10 . . . e3-e2

11 g5-g6

And now the black pawn gets home.

11 . . . e2-e1

Black has won!

The black pawn stands proudly on e1 to signal his victory. White's pawn on g6 is not far behind, but Black won because he got there first.

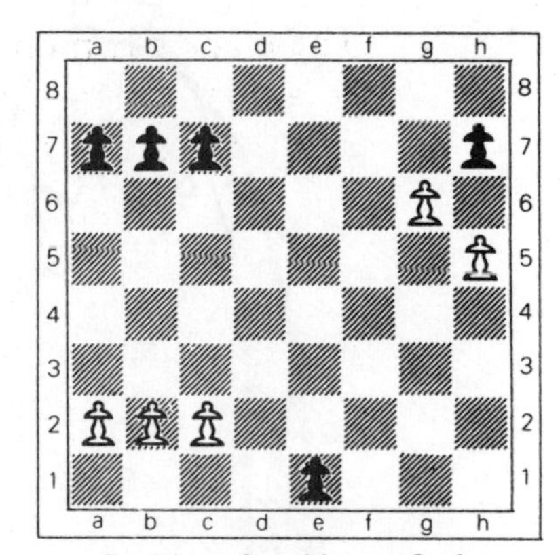

Position after 11 . . . e2-e1

Now you know the moves, have a go yourself. See if you can get a pawn to the other side of the board before your opponent.

The more games of Pawns you play the more you will get used to the way the pawn moves, and the sooner you will be able to play real chess well.

The King

The king was the most important person in the land. He may not have been the biggest or the strongest; he may not have been noble or brave; he may even have been weak and treacherous, but he was still king, the most important person. In chess, the king is not the most powerful piece, but, as we shall see, he is the most important.

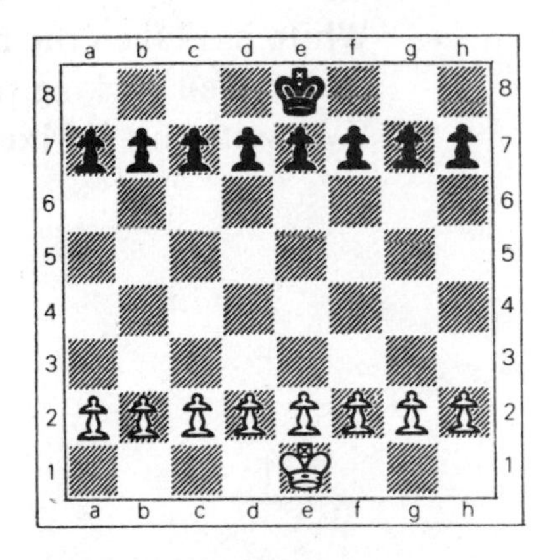

- ☐ **Each player has one king.**
- ☐ **The king begins the game on the e-file, behind the shield of pawns; the white king on e1, the black king on e8.**

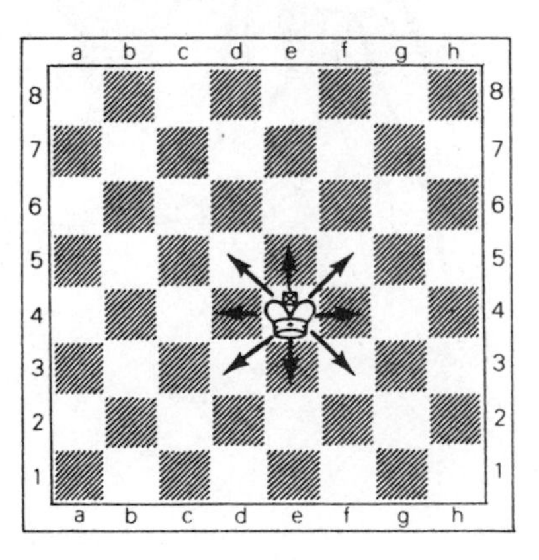

- ☐ **The king can move in any direction, backwards, forwards, sideways, or diagonally; but he can only move one square at a time.**

The king can move to any one of the eight squares marked with an arrow.

☐ **The king captures by making his normal move.**

The white king can move to e4.

There is a black pawn on e4, so the white king can capture him.

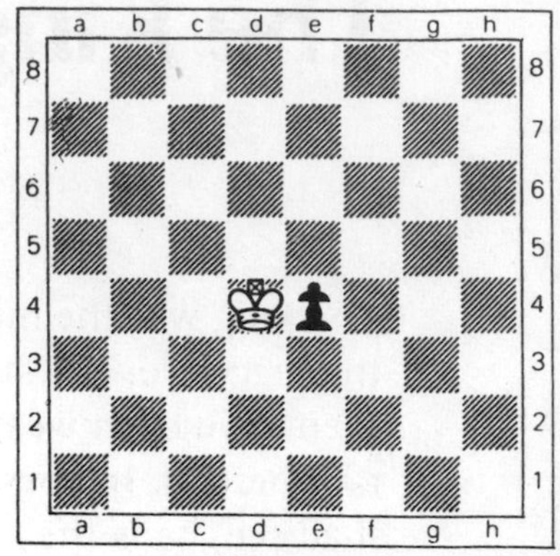
White to move

White has captured.

White has taken the black pawn off the board, and moved his king from d4 to e4.
(We write this **Kd4xe4**.)

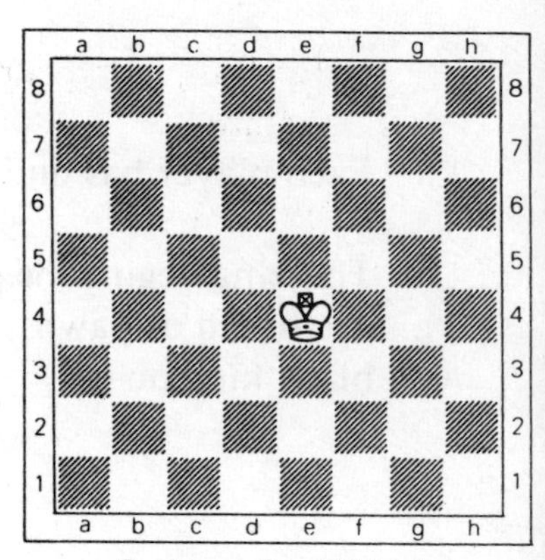
Position after Kd4xe4

☐ **A king must never move to a square where he is attacked.**

The white king cannot move to d5 or e5 because the black king is attacking those squares.

The white king cannot move to f4 because that square is attacked by the black pawn.

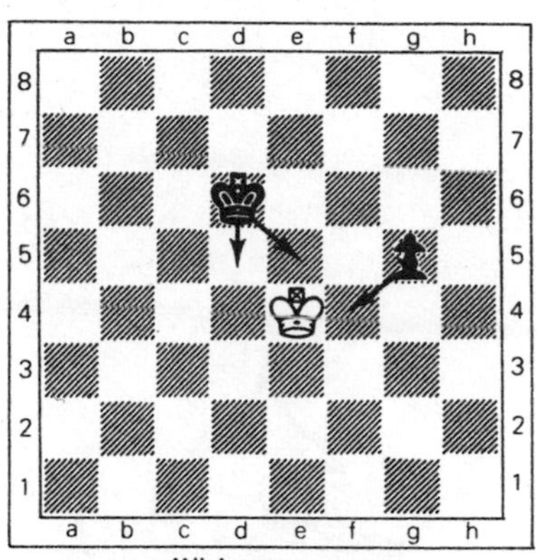

White to move

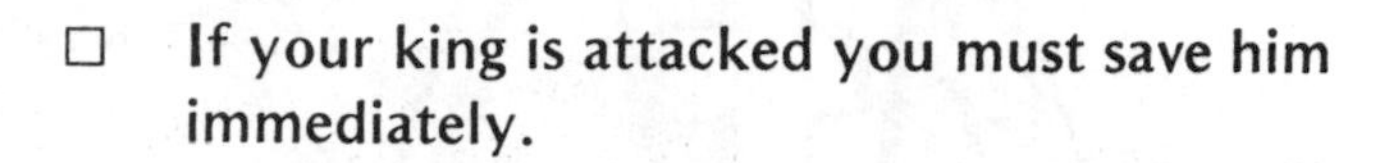

☐ **If your king is attacked you must save him immediately.**

The white king is attacked.
He can move to a5, b4, b3, or a3. Or he can take the black pawn.
The white pawn can also save his king by taking the black pawn.

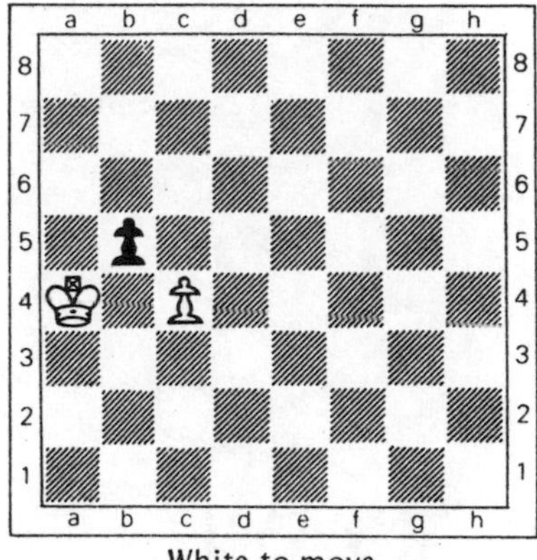

White to move

Remember what we said at the beginning: your king is the most important of your pieces.
You must never move your king to a square where he is attacked.
If your opponent threatens your king you must save him immediately.

Kings and Pawns
Set up your board like the diagram on the right.

Now you are ready for our second game.

We call this game 'Kings and Pawns'.

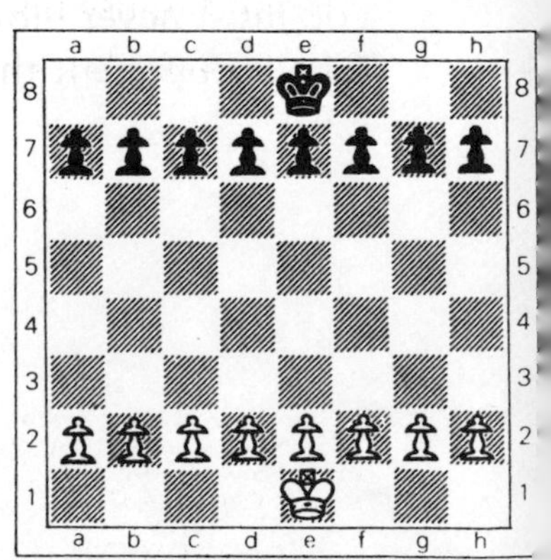

The game of Kings and Pawns

Your target in Kings and Pawns is just the same as it was in Pawns. The winner is the first player to get any *pawn* to the far end of the board.

Before you begin here are some hints:

Use your king to block enemy pawns.

If we were playing Pawns the black pawn on c4 would march merrily on to c1 and victory.

But now the white king on e1 can march across and cut him off.

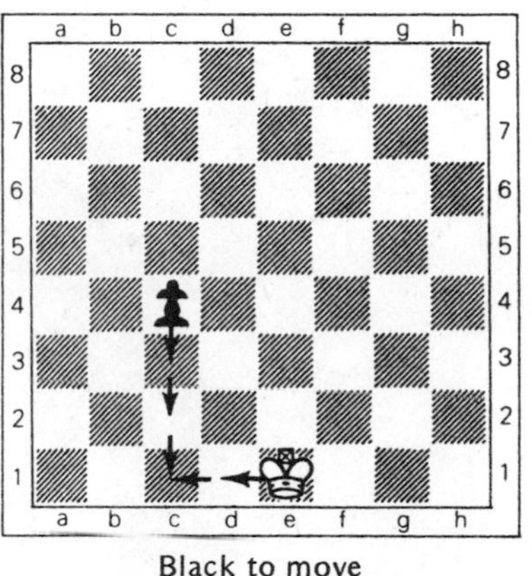

Black to move

Use your king to attack and defend.

White can use his king to attack.
White can play **Ke3-d4** to attack Black's pawn.

Black can use his king to defend.
Black can play . . . **Kb7-c6** and defend his pawn.

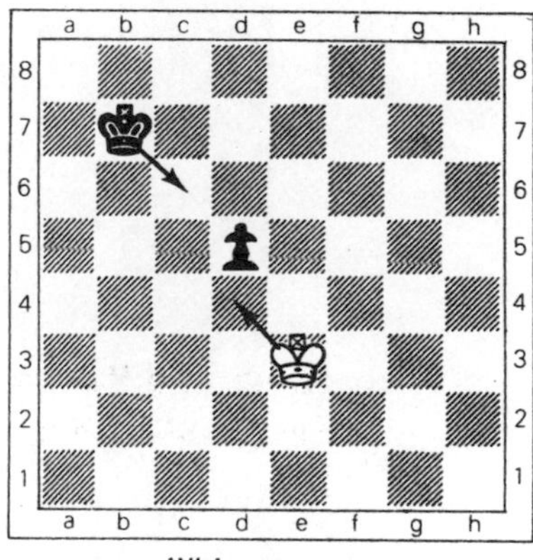

White to move

Now play a few games on your own. Remember, the more games you play, the more you will find out about the king and the pawns, the easier it will be to play proper chess later on.

The Queen

The queen is the most powerful chess piece; this is rather strange. Queen Boadicea may have led her troops in chopping up a few Romans, but power on the battlefield is not something for which ladies are famous. (Even Boadicea came to a miserable end when her army was foolish enough to attack Roman soldiers instead of Roman civilians!)

In the original Indian game of chess the piece was not called a queen, it was a wise man who stood beside the king at the start of the game and advised him. As a fighter the wise man was not very strong, so the chess piece was weak; he could only move diagonally one square at a time. When the game came to Europe the piece was given the new name of queen, probably because it stood next to the king and wasn't very strong! Later on, however, players decided that chess would be more fun if the army was stronger; with more powerful pieces the battles would be more exciting. So they changed the way in which the queen moved. In this way the queen, the lady of the chess-board, became the most powerful chess piece.

☐ **The queen can move in a straight line in any direction: backwards, forwards, sideways, or diagonally.**

☐ **The queen can move as many squares as she likes, but she cannot change direction in the middle of a move.**

The queen can move to any one of the squares marked with an arrow.

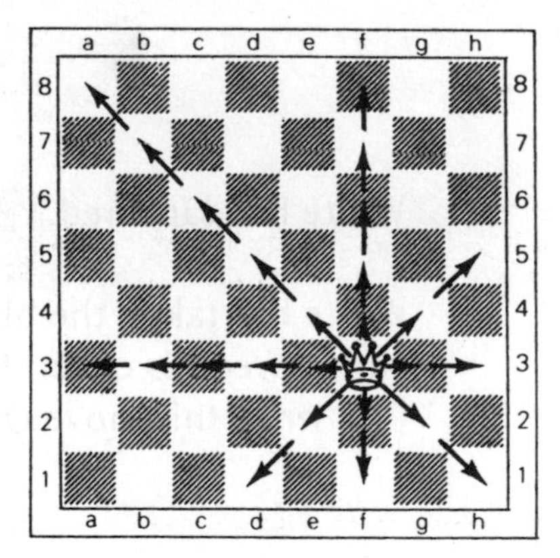

☐ **The queen cannot jump over pieces which stand in her way.**

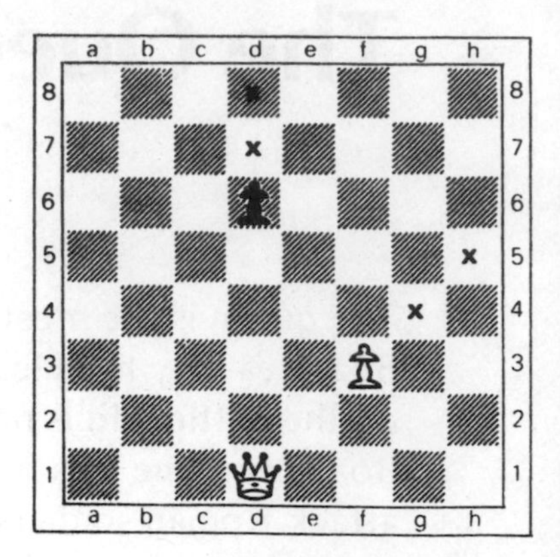

The white queen can move forward along the file from d1, but she cannot go to d7 or d8 because she cannot jump over the black pawn on d6.
The white queen cannot go to g4 or h5 because she cannot jump over the white pawn on f3.

☐ **The queen captures by making her normal move.**

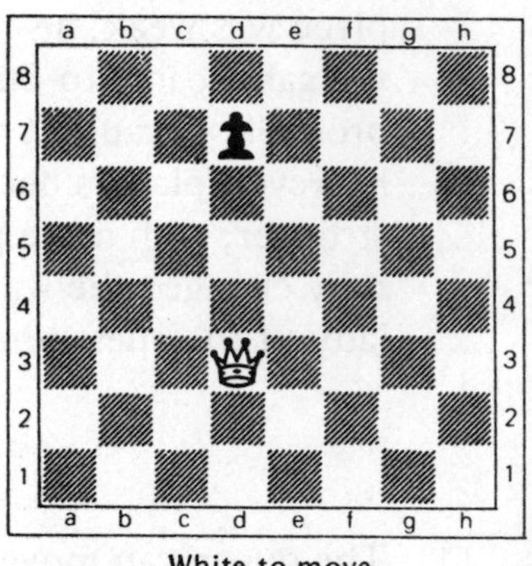
White to move

The white queen can move from d3 to d7.
So the white queen can capture the black pawn standing on d7.

White has captured.

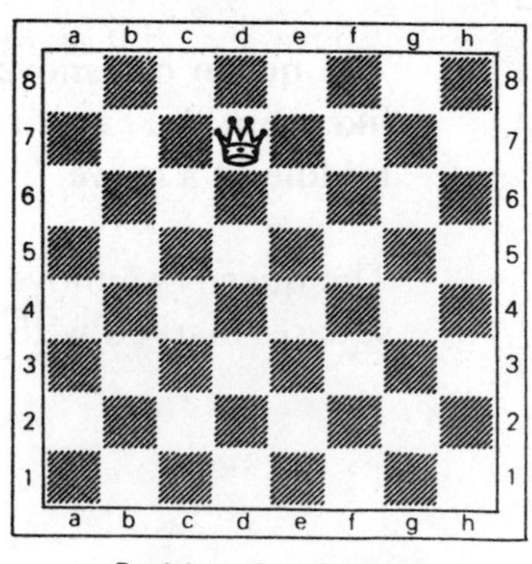
Position after Qd3xd7

White has taken the black pawn off the board, and moved his queen from d3 to d7.
(We write this move **Qd3xd7**.)

Now it's time for you to do some work!

Look at the diagram on the right.

How many black pawns can the white queen capture?

How many other moves can the white queen make?

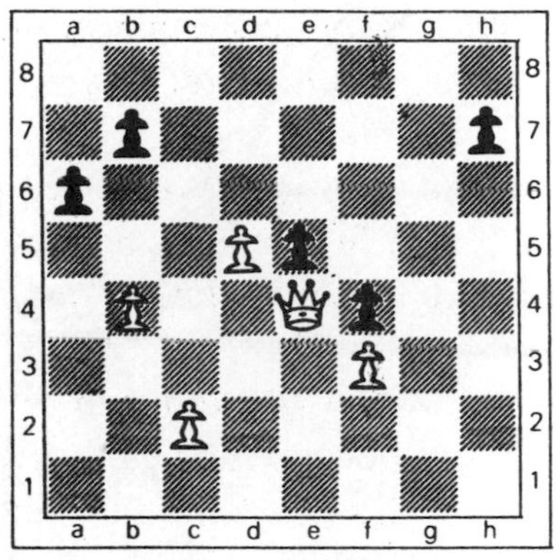

White to move

Three black pawns can be captured: those on e5, f4, and h7.

Eight other queen moves can be made: to c4, d4, d3, e3, e2, e1, f5, and g6.

Now, where would the white queen be in danger?
Can you find the squares on which the white queen could be taken?

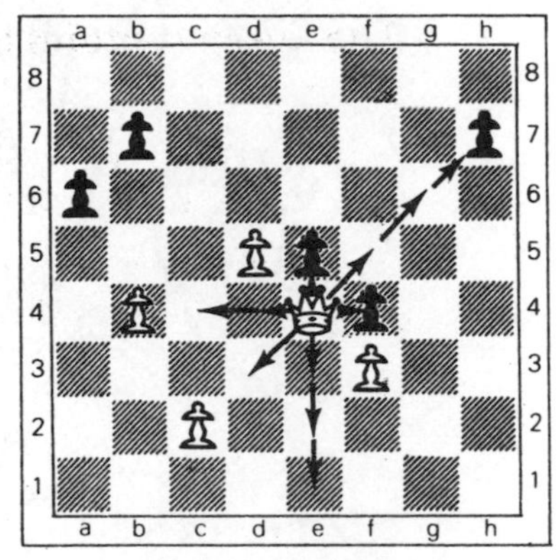

White to move

White does not want his powerful queen to be taken by a black pawn!

There are four bad queen moves.
If White moves his queen to d4, e3, or g6, or if he captures the black pawn on f4, then one of the black pawns will be able to take the white queen.

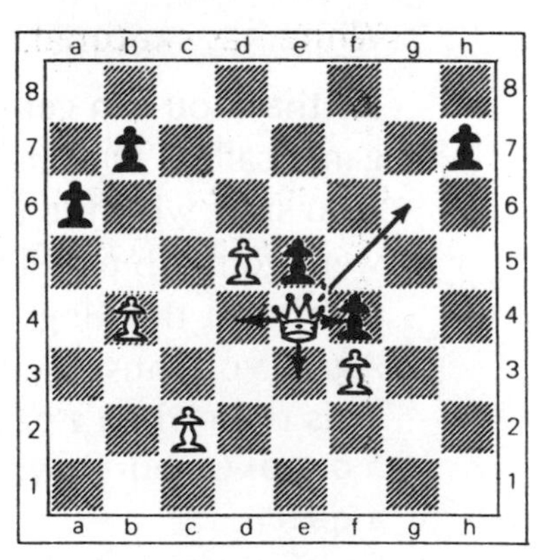

White to move

So that you can get used to the way the queen moves we will play a new game called 'Queens and Pawns'.
You start with the two rows of eight pawns facing each other, just as if you were going to play Pawns.
Don't put the kings on the board – we won't be needing them for this game.
Again you must try to get a pawn to the other end of the board.
This time when a pawn does get to the other end, the game does not stop.
You take your pawn off the board and put on the same square, in its place, a queen.
Go to the top of the next page, and you will see how it works.

White has a pawn on d7.

The white pawn can march on to the end of the board.

White moves his pawn forward one square:
1 d7-d8

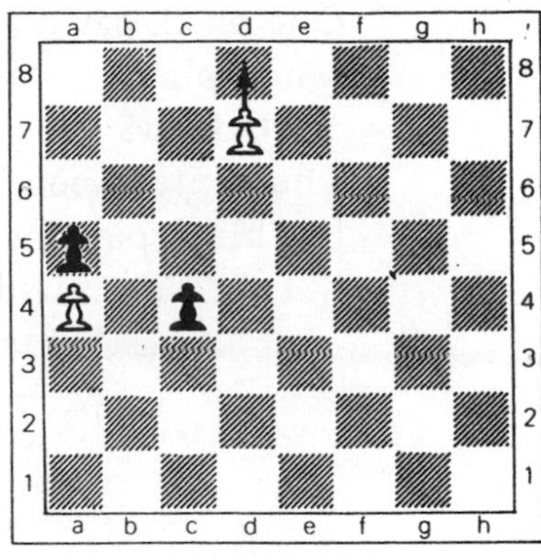

White to move

As soon as the pawn reaches d8 White takes it off the board, and puts his queen on d8 in its place.

The winner of Queens and Pawns is the player who is able to capture all his opponent's men.

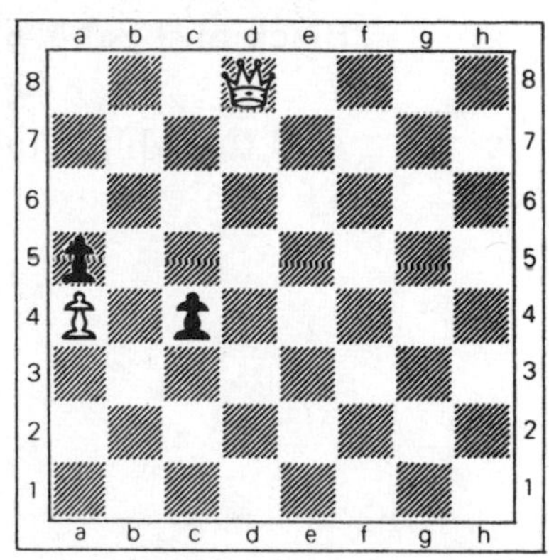

Position after 1 d7-d8 = queen

The white queen must now set out to catch the two black pawns.

It is Black's move; he can only move one of his pawns, so he plays:
1 ... c4-c3
Now the white queen is ready to show her strength.

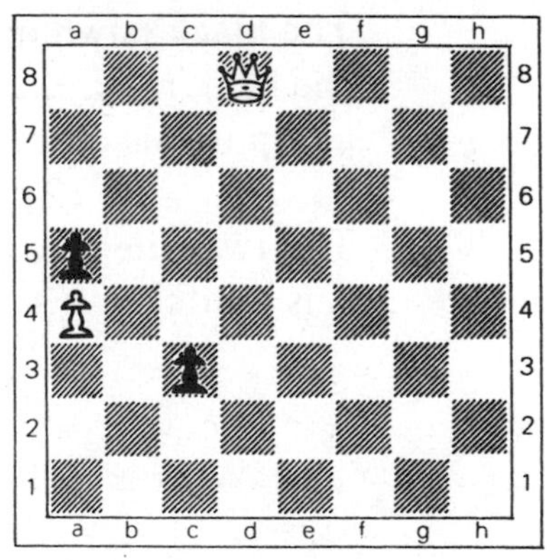

Postion after 1 ... c4-c3

One black pawn is already doomed!
White plays:
2 Qd8xa5
The white queen is like a cat after mice. The last black pawn will try to scamper home, but the queen will be too quick for him.

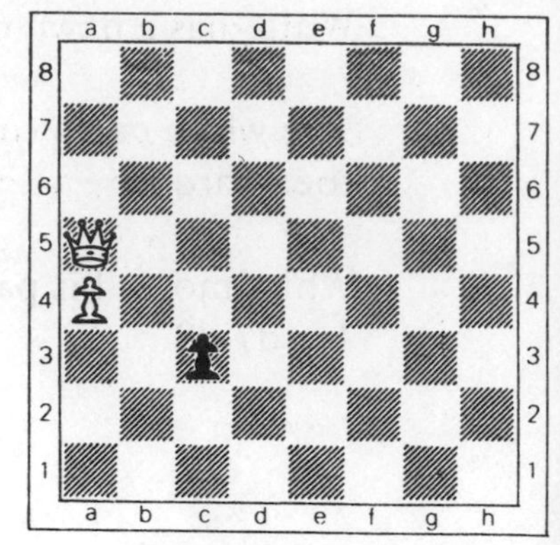
Position after 2 Qd8xa5

Black pushes his pawn on:
2 . . . c3-c2
And the white queen swings into the attack:
3 Qa5-c5

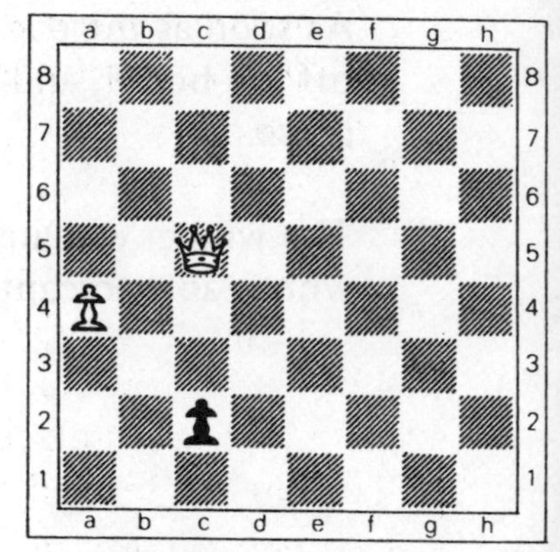
Position after 3 Qa5-c5

The black pawn marches on again and reaches the back rank. Black takes him off the board, and puts his queen on in his place:
3 . . . c2-c1 = queen
The two queens are attacking each other, but it is White's move.

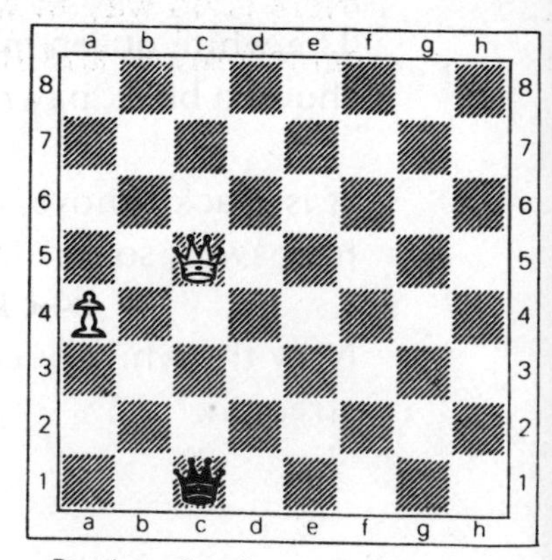
Postion after 3 . . . c2-c1 = queen

White strikes first:
4 Qc5xc1
Black has run out of men!
He has lost them all.
White has won.

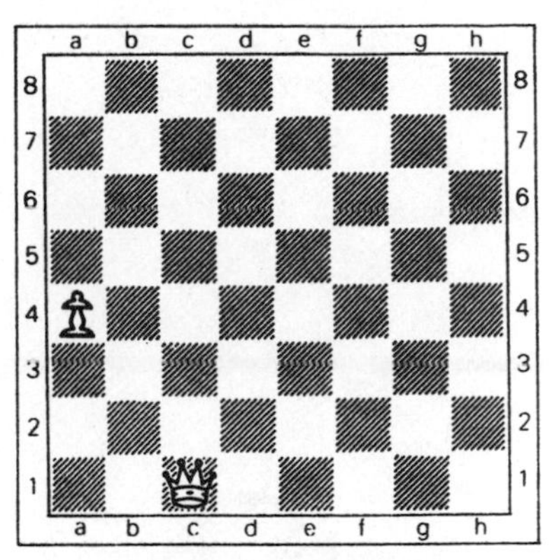

Position after 4 Qc5xc1

Now you can see why the queen is so powerful; she can spring around the board backwards and forwards and from side to side, while the poor pawns can only plod steadily on. Play a few games of Queens and Pawns of your own; you will learn quickly how to handle the queen, and discover just how strong she can be.

Remember, for Queens and Pawns you start just the same as for Pawns. When you get a pawn to the other end you take him off the board and put a queen in his place. If you get a second pawn to the other end, then you can have a second queen. Try to capture all of your opponent's army; when he has run out of men you have won.

Sometimes you may reach a position where both sides have a queen and there is no way in which either player can win. Then you must call the game a draw, and start again!

Check

When a king is attacked we say he is in **check.** Look at the two positions below.

The white pawn on e4 is attacking the black king.

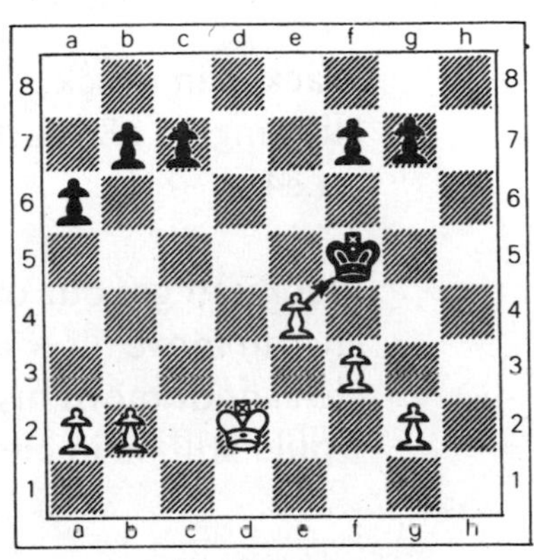
Black to move

Black is in *check* from the white pawn.

The black queen on g6 is attacking the white king.

White is in *check* from the black queen.

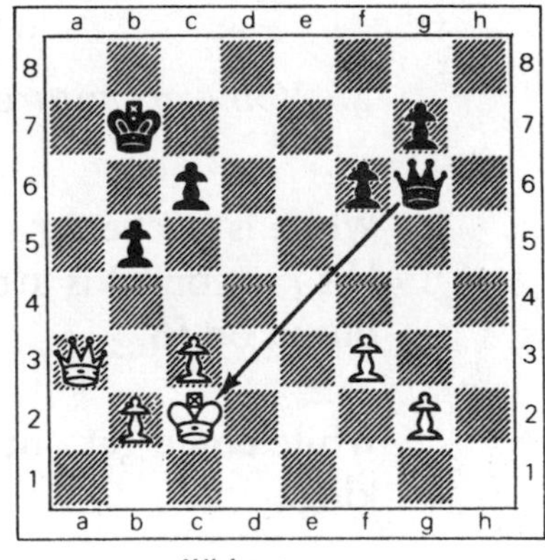
White to move

Usually, when you attack the enemy king, you tell your opponent by saying 'Check' as you make your move.
You don't have to say check, but it is polite to do so. You don't win games or friends by being unsporting; so get into the habit straight away!

- ☐ **You must never allow your king to be taken.**
- ☐ **When you are in check you must get out of check straight away. You have no choice; you must spend your next move getting out of check.**

There are three ways of escaping from check.

1. *You can move your king to a square where he is not attacked.*

Black is in check.
His king on a8 is attacked by the white queen on e4.

Black can get out of check by moving his king.
He can move his king to a7 or b8.
He cannot move his king to b7 because he would still be in check from the white queen.

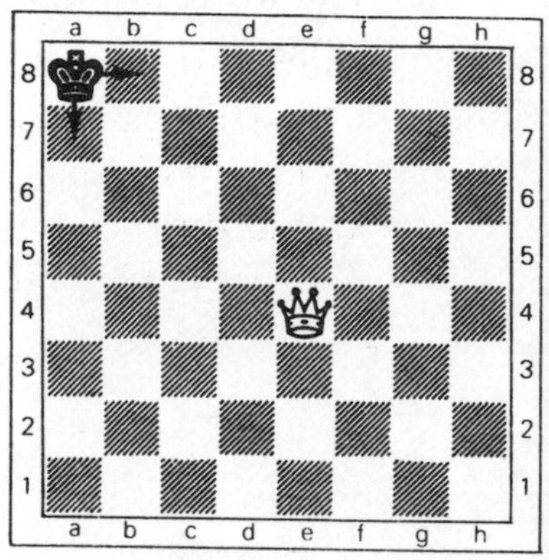

Black to move

2. *You can capture the piece attacking your king.*

White is in check.
His king on c3 is attacked by the black queen on f6.

White could get out of check by moving his king.

White can also get out of check by capturing the black queen.
The white pawn on g5 is attacking the black queen.
If the pawn captures the queen White will no longer be in check.

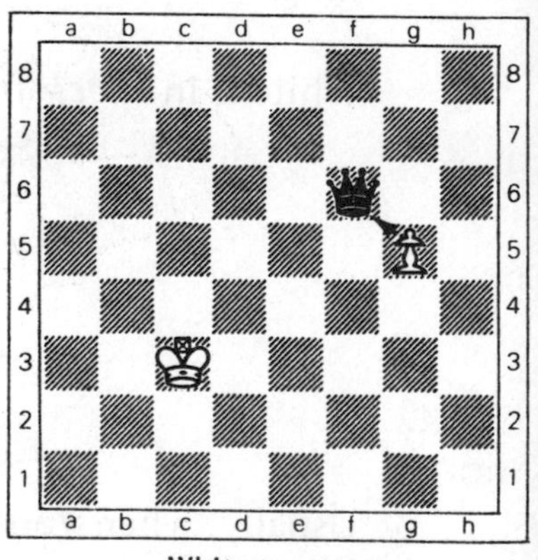

White to move

3. *You can block the line of check by putting a piece in the way.*

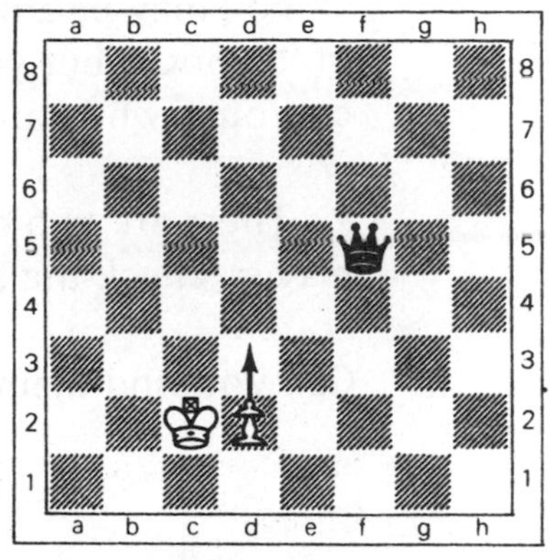
White to move

White is in check.
His king on c2 is attacked by the black queen on f5.

White could get out of check by moving his king.

White can also get out of check by blocking the line between the black queen and his king.
The white pawn on d2 can move forward one square to d3.
On d3 the pawn blocks the line of check.
The white king hides safely behind the pawn.

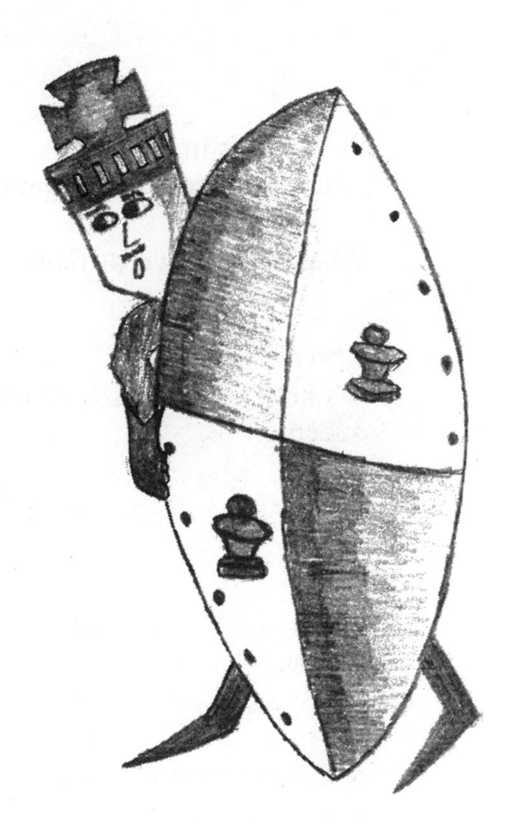

Now test what you have learnt by doing a little quiz. You will find the answers on page 135 at the back of the book.

You may be able to answer the questions by just looking at the diagrams in the book, but you will probably find it easier if you set up the positions on your own board.

1. There are two different moves White can play to check the black king.

Can you find them both?

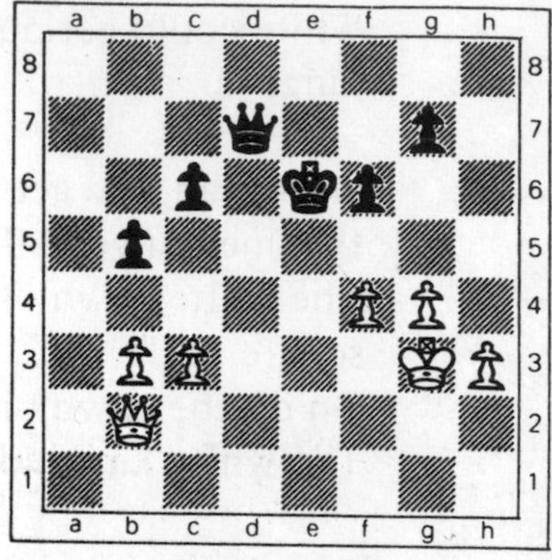

White to move

2. Black is in check.
Black has two ways to get out of check.

What are the two different moves?

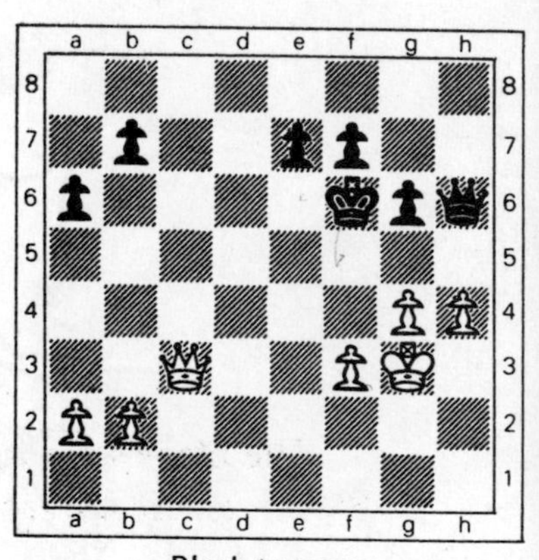

Black to move

3. Black has two different moves with his queen which will check the white king. Can you find them?

One of these two moves would be very bad.

Can you see why?

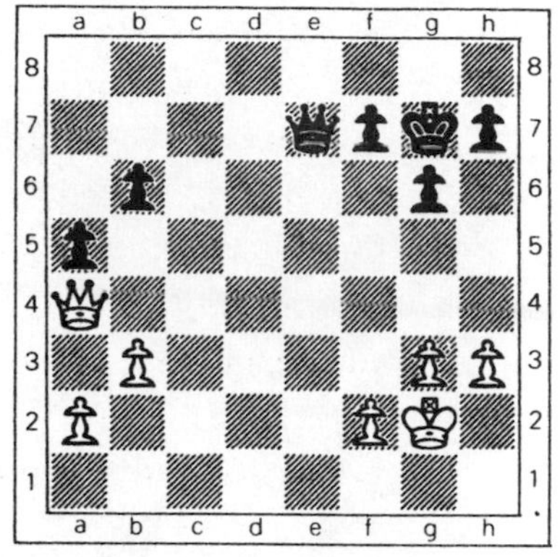

Black to move

4. The white king is in check. Can White get out of check by taking the black pawn on d4?

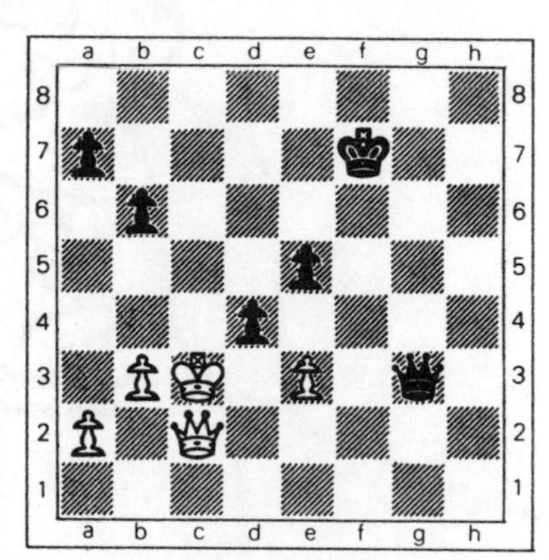

White to move

5. The black king is in check. Black can escape from check in eight ways.

See if you can find all eight moves Black can play.

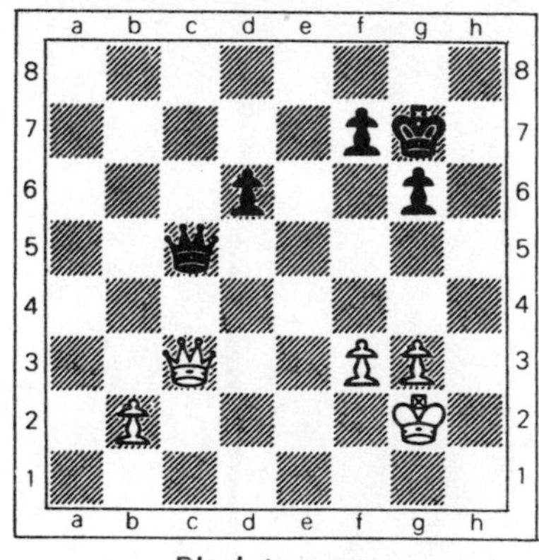

Black to move

Checkmate

When your king is in check you must get out of check.
But suppose you can't get out of check?

Suppose that your king is in check.
Suppose that wherever you move your king he is still in check.
Suppose that you cannot capture the piece that is attacking your king.
Suppose that you cannot put anything in the way to block the check.
No matter what you do you cannot get out of check.

Black is in check. His king is attacked by White's queen.

There is no safe square to which his king can run.

He cannot capture the white queen.

He cannot block the queen's line of attack.

Black cannot get out of check.

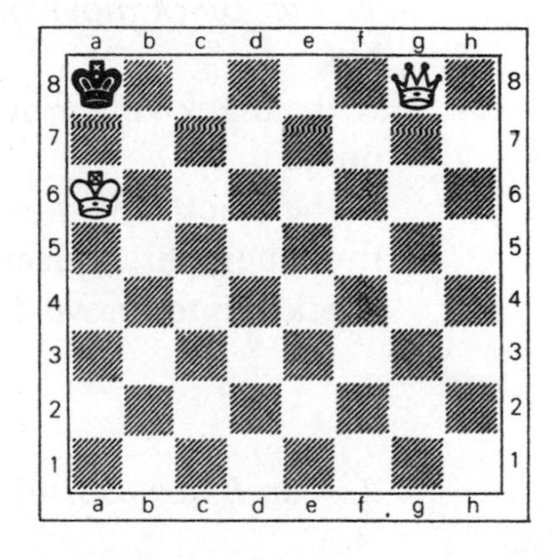

When a king cannot escape from check we say he is **checkmated.** This is what you will be trying to do in a game of chess. You will be trying to get your opponent's king in checkmate. You will be trying to attack his king in such a way that he cannot escape. The player who gets checkmate has executed his opponent's king; the game is over, and he has won.

Understanding checkmate is so important that we will spend some more time just making sure that you have really got the idea.

The black king is in check; he is attacked by the white queen on h8.

Can Black save his king, can he get out of check?

There are three ways he can try; let's look at them in turn.

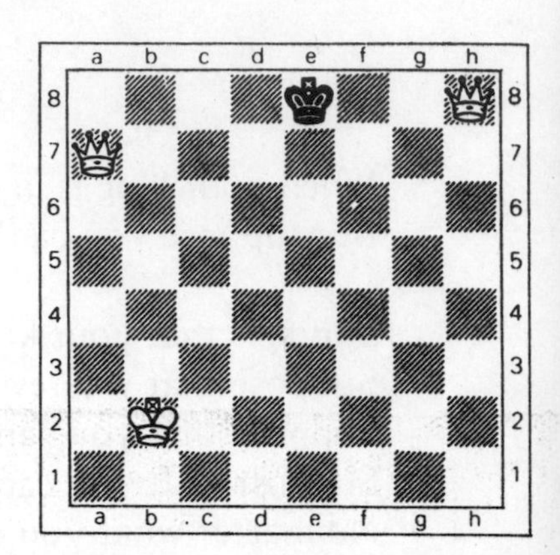

1. *Can Black move his king?*
No.
If the black king moves to f8 or d8, he is still in check from the white queen on h8.
If the black king moves forward, to d7, e7, or f7, then he is in check from the other white queen.
Black cannot move his king to get out of check.

2. *Can Black capture the white queen?*
No.
The black king is too far away from the white queen to take her.
Black cannot get out of check by capturing.

3. *Can Black block the line of check?*
No.
Black only has a king; so he has nothing he can put in the way.
Black cannot block the check.

All three ways are useless. Black cannot get out of check. He cannot save his king. It is checkmate. White has won.

Look at some more examples:

Black is in check.
There is no safe square to which his king can escape.
He cannot take the white queen because she is defended.
He cannot block the check.
He cannot get out of check.

Checkmate!

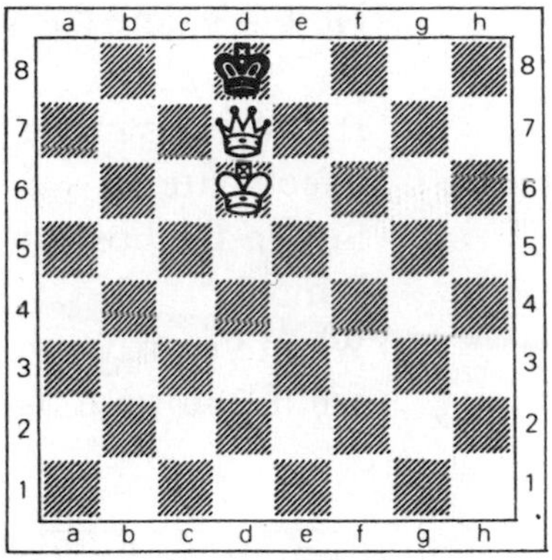

Checkmate

It is Black's turn to move.
He moves his queen from d6 to d1 and says check. (. . . **Qd6-d1+**)
White cannot get out of check.
None of the three ways of trying is any good to him.

Checkmate!

. . . Qd6-d1 mate

It is White's turn to move.
He moves his queen from a7, captures the black pawn on g7, and says check. (**Qa7xg7+**)
Black cannot get out of check.

Checkmate!

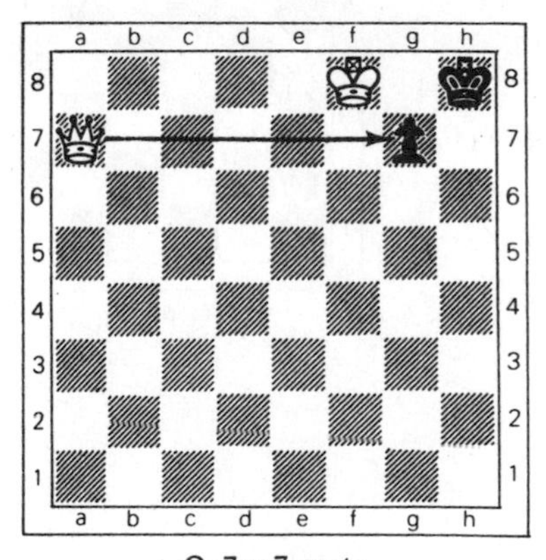

Qa7xg7 mate

Now it's time for you to do some more work; here is another quiz.

It is White's move in each position below. With his first move White can get checkmate.
Set up the postion on your board and see. Can you find the right move for White?
When you have worked out the move look for the answers on page 135 and see if you were right.

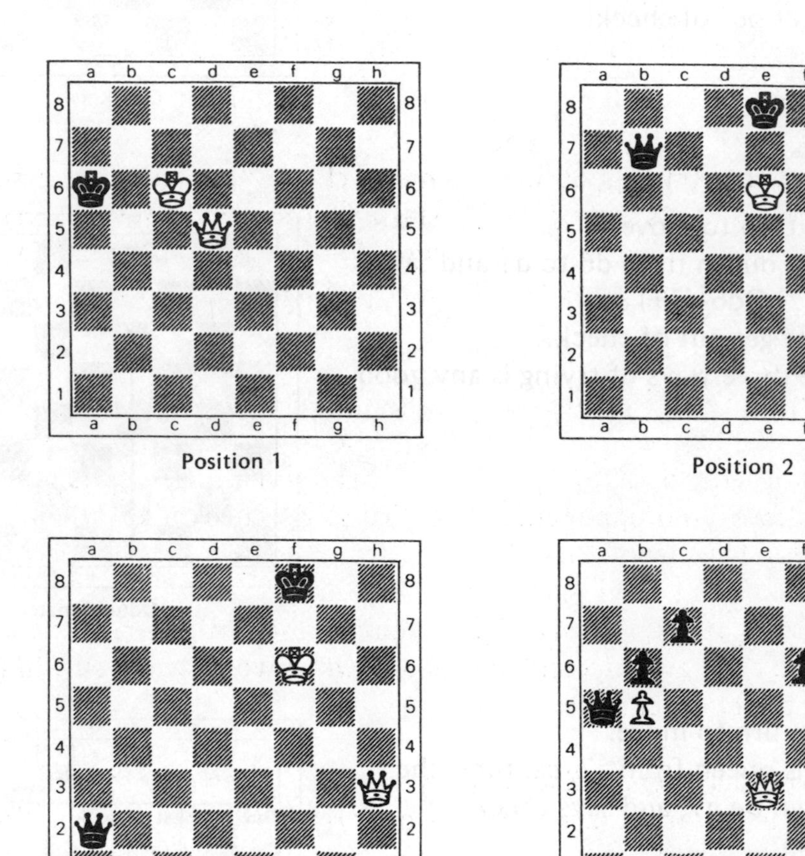

Position 1

Position 2

Position 3

Position 4

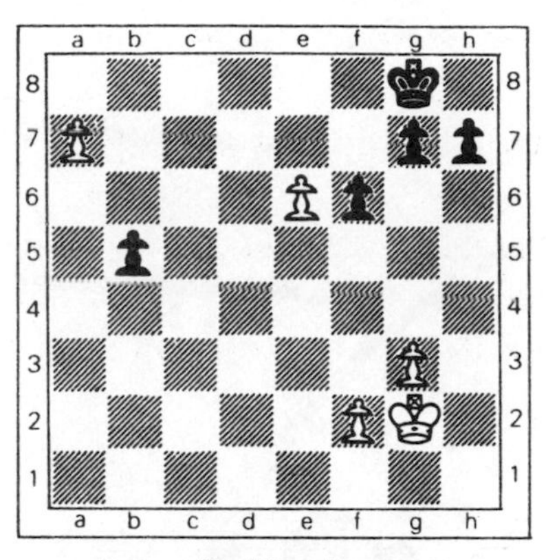

Position 5

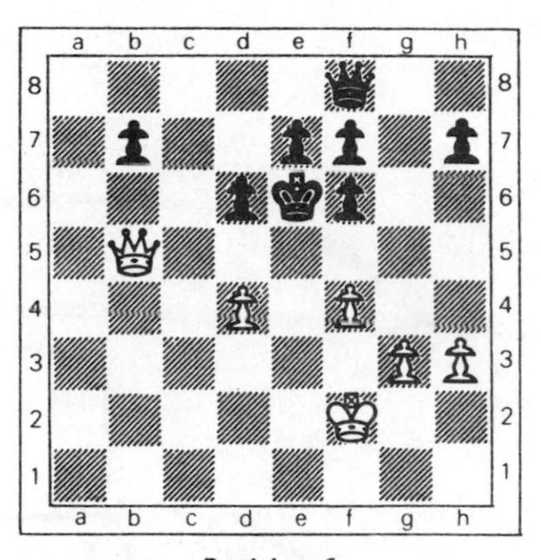

Position 6

When you get checkmate, you win a game of chess. Now you must practise getting checkmate for yourself. If you started with a whole set of chess-men, you would find it difficult to get checkmate. So let us do it the easy way to begin with, by playing a game called 'Catch the King'.

Catch the King

Start with the kings and pawns, just as if you were going to play Kings and Pawns. First try to get a pawn to the other end of the board. When you get a pawn to the other end, take it off the board and put a queen in its place. Now try to catch your opponent's king. Try to get checkmate. When you get checkmate you have won.

Before you start here's one small tip. If you get a second pawn to the end of the board you can have a second queen, and with two queens you will find it much easier to get checkmate.

Of course your opponent will also be trying to get a pawn to the other end. He will be trying to get a queen. He will be trying to checkmate you! You must stop him. Don't forget you can use your queen to capture his pawns, as well as to attack his king.

Now off you go and try to catch that king!

Stalemate

When you were playing 'Catch the King' did you ever reach a position where one side was not in check but couldn't move? Perhaps you had a position like the one below:

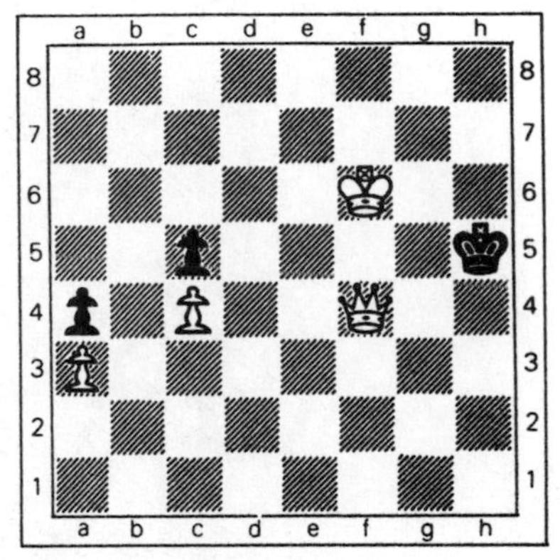
Black to move

If it were White's move, it would be easy. White would play **Qf4-g5 checkmate.**

But it is Black's move!

What can Black do?
Nothing!
Black cannot move his king because he would be in check wherever he moved.
Black cannot move his pawns because they are blocked.

Black is not in check, so it cannot be checkmate. It is his move, yet there is nowhere he can go. What happens now?

□ **When it is one player's turn to move, and he is not in check, and there is no possible move he can make, the position is called 'Stalemate' and the game ends as a draw.**

This is a new rule for your game of Catch the King. Remember, when you are trying to get checkmate, that your opponent will escape with a draw if he can reach a stalemate position.

STEP 8

The Rook

A rook was a chariot in the original Indian game of chess; it was a platform on wheels surrounded by a wooden wall to protect a soldier who stood inside. Probably in the early Indian chess-sets there was a wooden horse to pull it along! As the game spread to Europe the piece became simpler; it lost its wheels and the soldier; it became a small round tower with battlements, just like a corner tower in a castle wall. Sometimes people actually call the piece a castle, but its proper name comes from the Persian word 'rukh', meaning a chariot.

☐ **Each player has two rooks.**

☐ **The rooks begin the game at the corners of the board, the white rooks at a1 and h1, and the black rooks at a8 and h8.**

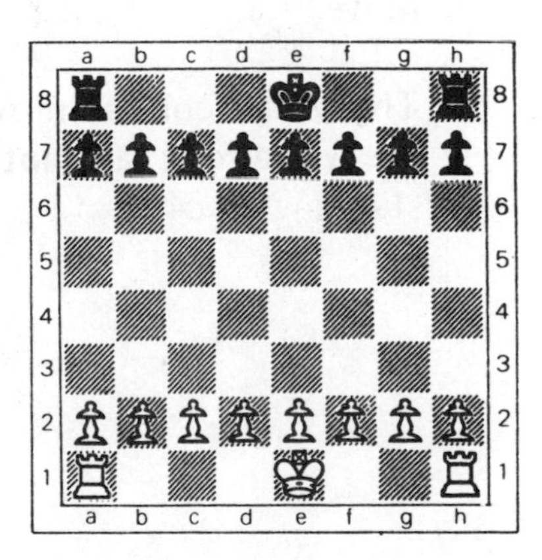

☐ **The rook can move in a straight line backwards, forwards, or sideways.**

☐ **The rook can move as many squares as he likes, but he cannot change direction in the middle of a move.**

The rook can move to any one of the squares marked with an arrow.

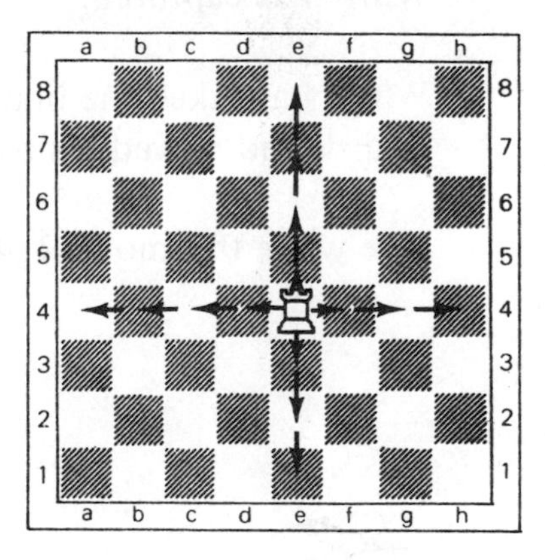

☐ **The rook cannot jump over pieces which stand in his way.**

The white rook can move forward along the file from c1, but he cannot go to c6, c7, or c8, because he cannot jump over the black pawn on c5.

The white rook cannot go to g1 or h1 because he cannot jump over the white king on f1.

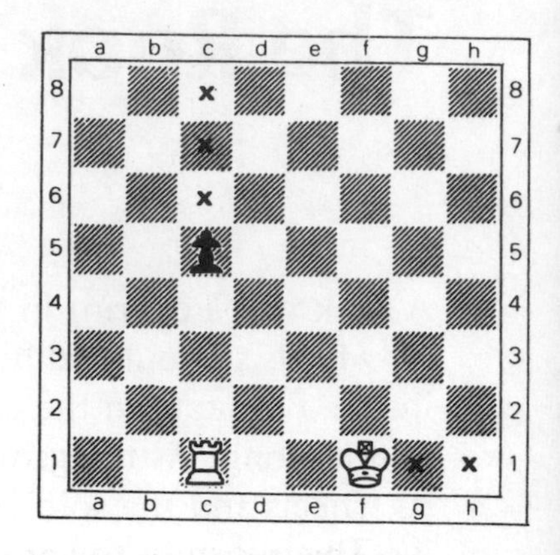

☐ **The rook captures by making his normal move.**

The white rook can move from g4 to c4. So the white rook can capture the black queen standing on c4.

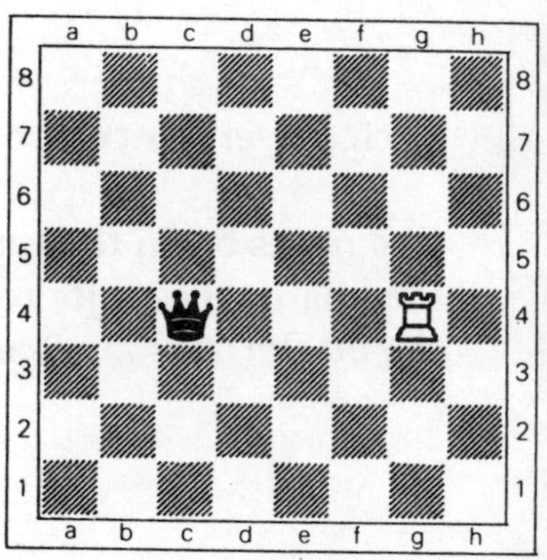

White to move

White has captured.

White has taken the black queen off the board, and moved his rook from g4 to c4.

(We write this move **Rg4xc4.**)

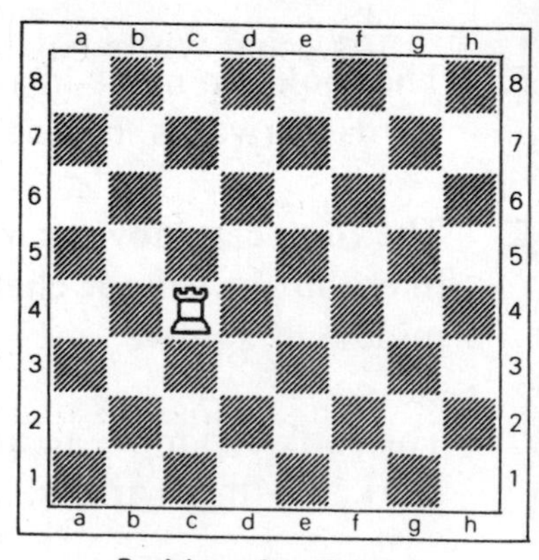

Position after Rg4xc4

Mini-Chess

Now we are going to take a real step towards real chess by playing a game called 'Mini-Chess'. For this game you will need all the men we have met in the book so far. You already know where to put the kings, the pawns, and the rooks, ready for the start of the game, and now we will see where the queen goes.

☐ **Each player has one queen.**

☐ **The queen begins the game next to her king, the white queen on d1, and the black queen on d8.**

This is easy to remember; the white queen stands on a white square, and the black queen on a black square.

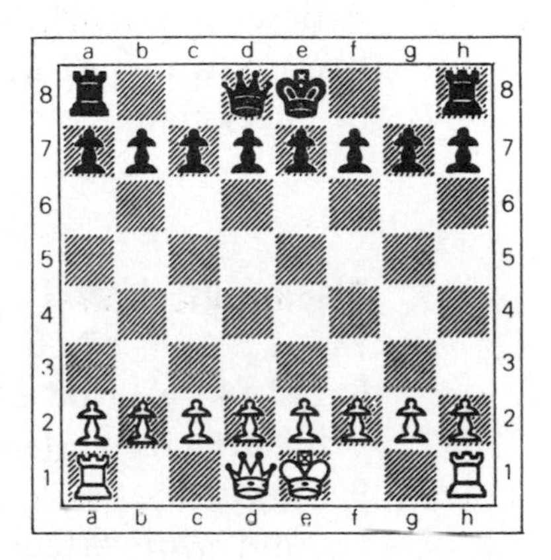

Set your board up like the diagram above and you are ready for a game of Mini-Chess. Your aim is to checkmate the enemy king.

Let us look at a game of Mini-Chess to see how it works.

As usual White begins:

1 e2-e4 c7-c6

2 Qd1-g4

White brings out his queen to attack the black pawn on g7.

2 . . . g7-g6

3 h2-h4 Qd8-b6

Black brings his queen out to attack a pawn, the white one on b2.

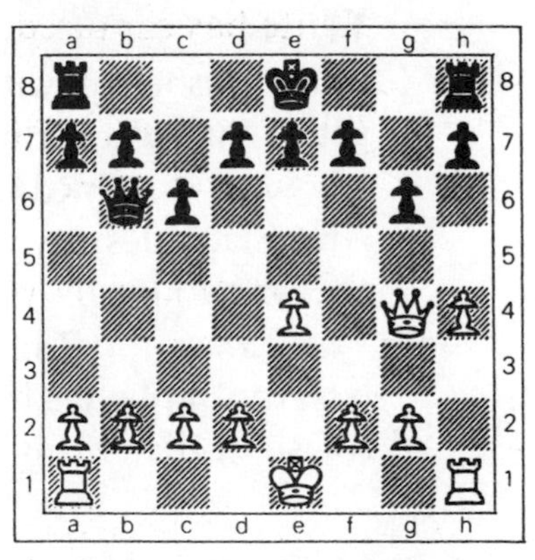

Position after 3 . . . Qd8-b6

4 b2-b3 d7-d5
5 Rh1-h3
White wants to bring his rook into the attack.
5 . . . d5xe4
6 Qg4xe4 Ra8-d8
Black moves his rook to fire at the enemy lines along the d-file.
7 Rh3-e3
A fierce move! White threatens to capture the black pawn on e7 with his queen. That would be checkmate!

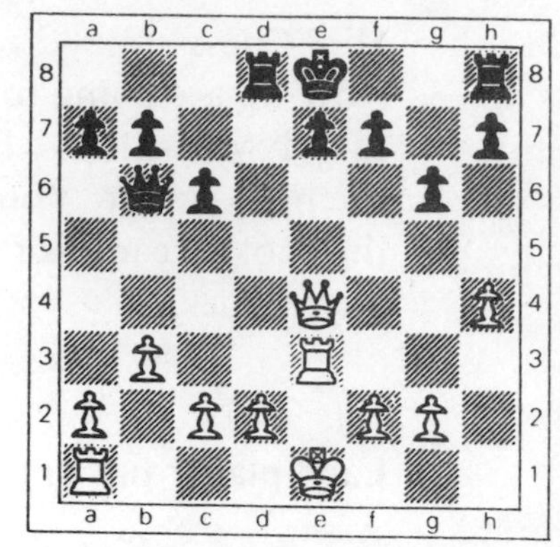
Position after 7 Rh3-e3

Black must defend:
7 . . . e7-e6
8 f2-f4 Rd8-d4
Black attacks White's queen . . .
9 Qe4-e5
. . . and White attacks Black's other rook.
9 . . . Rh8-f8
10 g2-g4 Qb6-d8
The queen joins the rook in attack on the d-file.

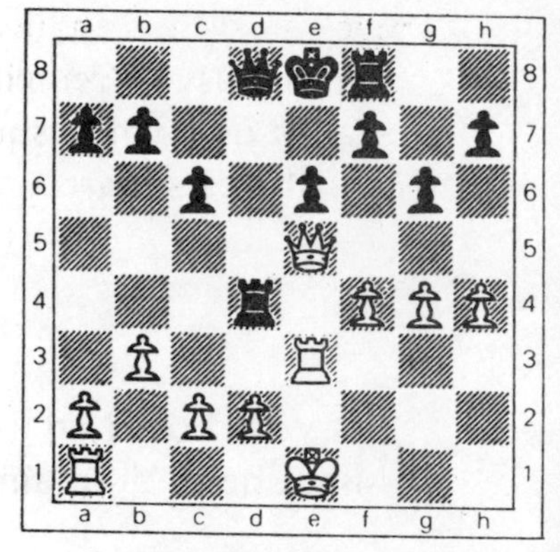
Position after 10 . . . Qb6-d8

11 f4-f5
White pushes on with his attack; he wants to get at that black king!
11 . . . Rd4xd2
And Black destroys one of the guards around the white king.
12 f5xe6 Rd2xc2
Now both players have their pieces ready to smash at the enemy king.

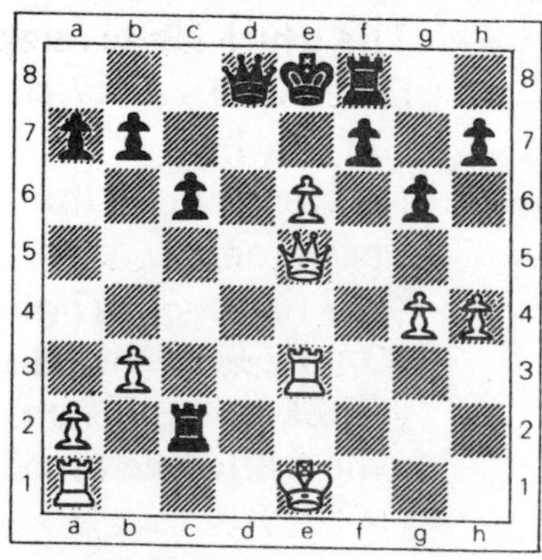
Position after 12 . . . Rd2xc2

13 e6xf7+
The black king is in trouble! He is attacked by both the white pawn and the white queen.
13 . . . Ke8xf7
14 Ra1-d1
White brings his other rook into the attack and threatens the black queen.
However, he gives his opponent the chance to fight back.

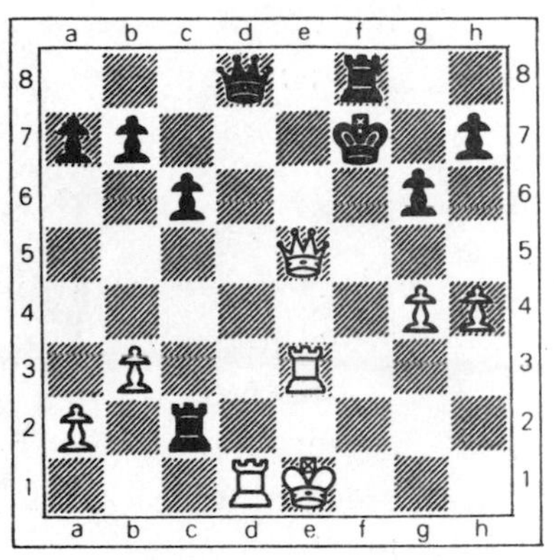

Position after 14 Ra1-d1

Black seizes his chance:
14 . . . Qd8xh4+
15 Qe5-g3
White blocks the check.
15 . . . Qh4-h1+
Now White must give away his queen . . .
16 Qg3-g1
. . . but he still can't stop checkmate.
16 . . . Qh1xg1 mate

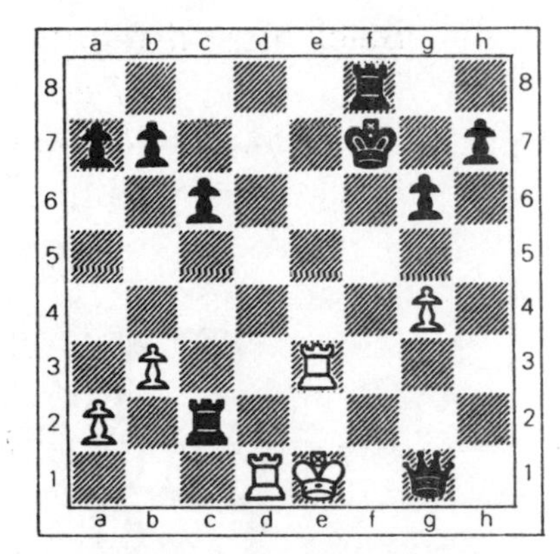

Position after 16 . . . Qh1xg1 checkmate

The white king is trapped; there is no escape; Black has won; Black has got checkmate.

Now play a few games of your own. You know how your pieces can move; so use them to attack the enemy. You may find it easier if you can weaken your opponent's army by winning some of his pieces. You may find it helps if you can strengthen your own army by marching a pawn through to the far end of the board and getting a second queen . . . or even a third! But, whatever you do, never forget that it is the enemy king that is your target; it is checkmate that is your aim. *And* don't forget that your opponent has the same ideas about attacking your king!

STEP 9

Castling

You probably learnt quite a few things playing Mini-Chess. Did you notice how difficult it is to attack a king when he is hiding behind a shield of pawns, and how much easier it is to attack him when he is out in the open and you can get at him? Did you notice how difficult it is to attack with just one piece, and how much stronger your army becomes when you have several pieces fighting together?

There is a special move which you are allowed to play only once in a game of chess; it can help you by putting your king safely behind a wall of pawns, and by joining your rooks so that they can work together. This special move is called **castling**.

This is a position before White has castled. His king is in the open, his rook stuck in the corner.

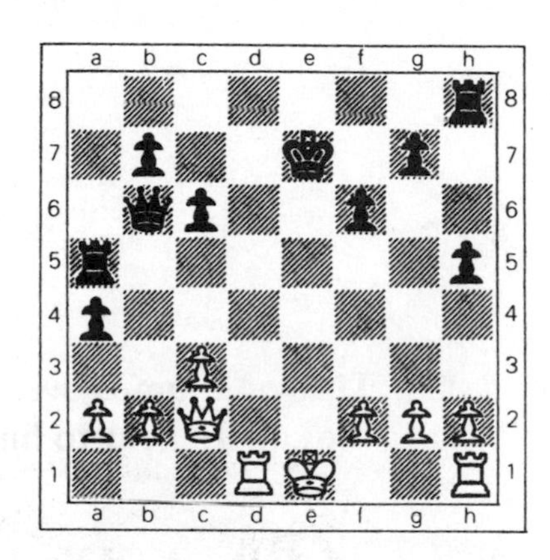

This is the same position after White has castled. His king is tucked away safely behind a line of pawns; his rook has joined its partner in the middle.

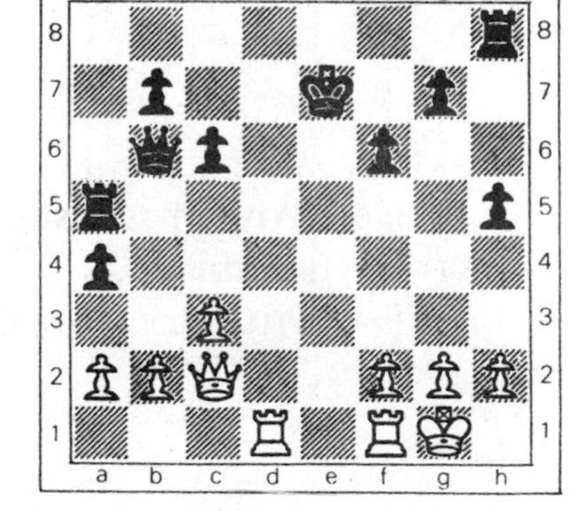

Now turn over and you will learn the rules for castling.

Castling is one move using two of the pieces, the king and either of the rooks.

There are several rules.

☐ **The king and the rook must be on their original squares.**

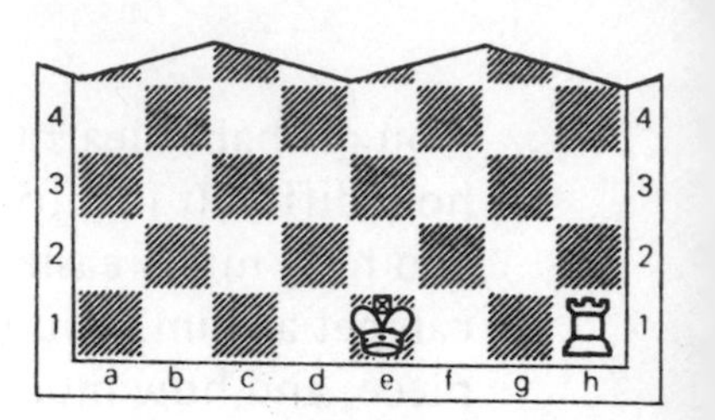

☐ **The king moves two squares sideways towards the rook.**

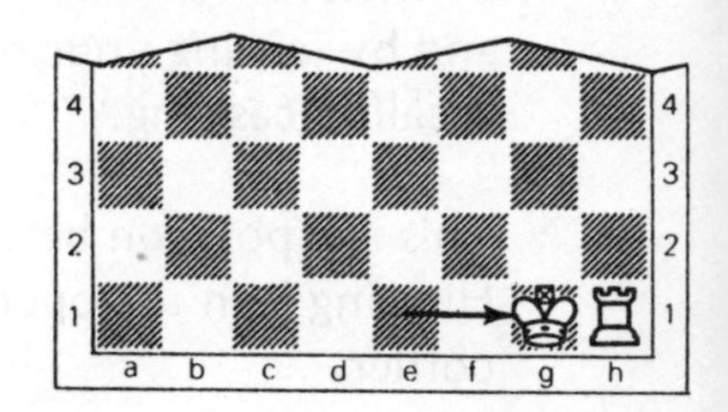

☐ **The rook jumps over the king and lands on the square next to him.**

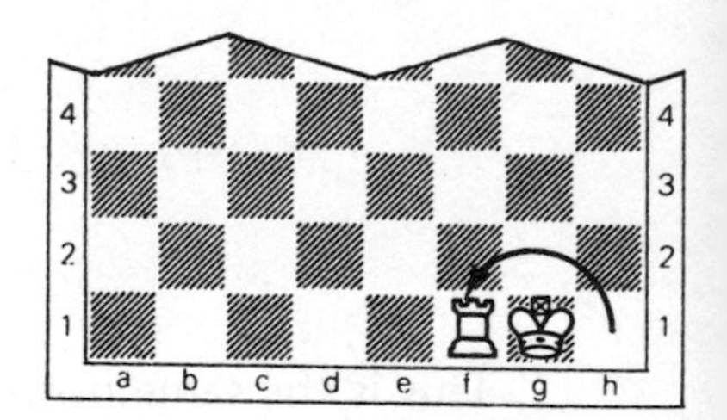

Here White has castled on the King's side of the board.
(We write this move **0-0**.)

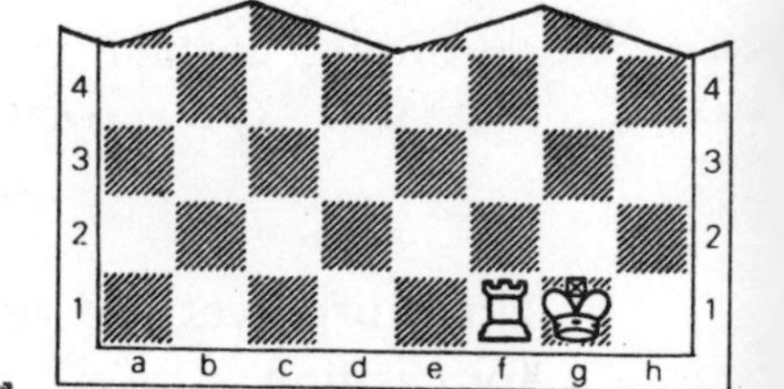

You may also castle on the Queen's side of the board. The rules are exactly the same.

The king and rook must still be on their original squares.

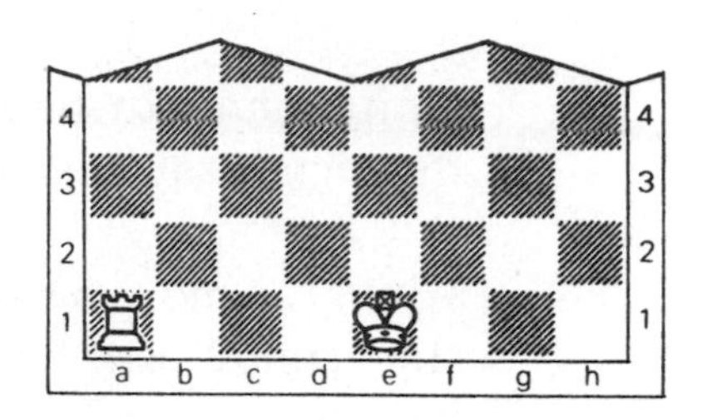

The king moves two squares towards the rook.

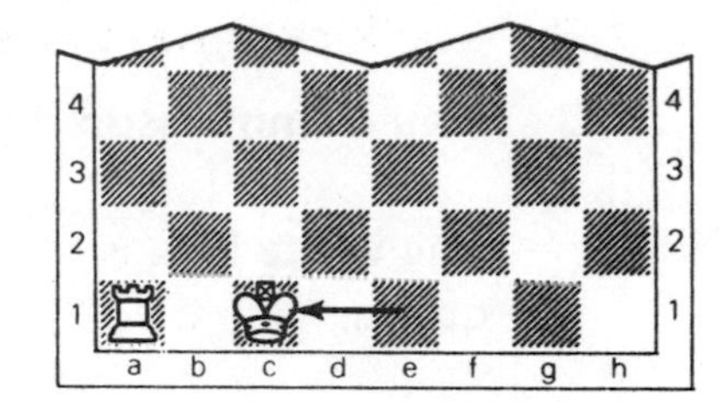

The rook jumps over the king and lands on the square next to him.

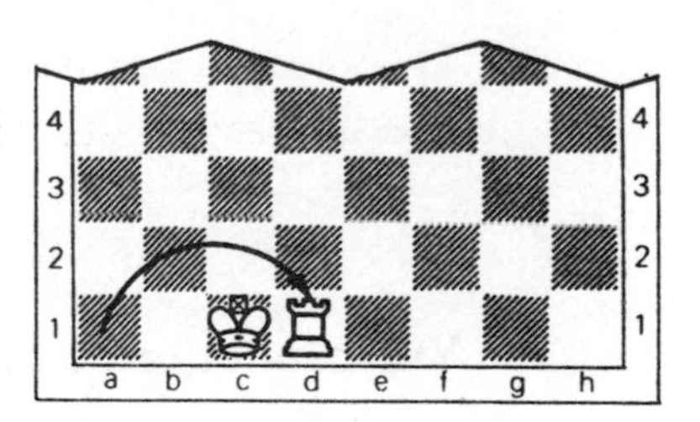

White has castled on the Queen's side. (We write this move **0-0-0**.)

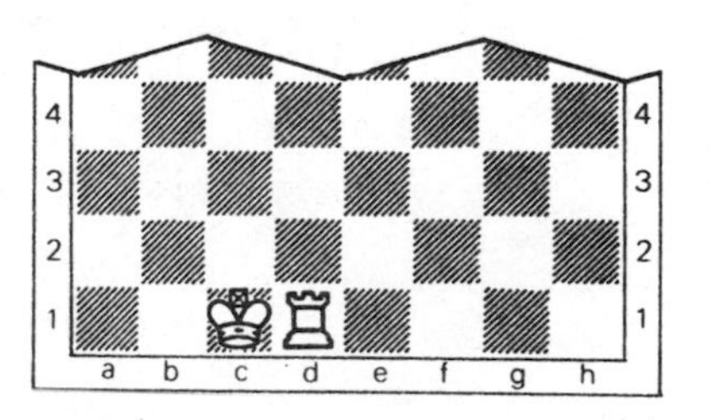

Now here are some more rules, about when you cannot castle.

☐ **You cannot castle if you have already moved either your king or the rook you are using.**

White cannot castle because his rook is not on its original square.

White can move his rook back to a1, but he still cannot castle because his rook has already moved.

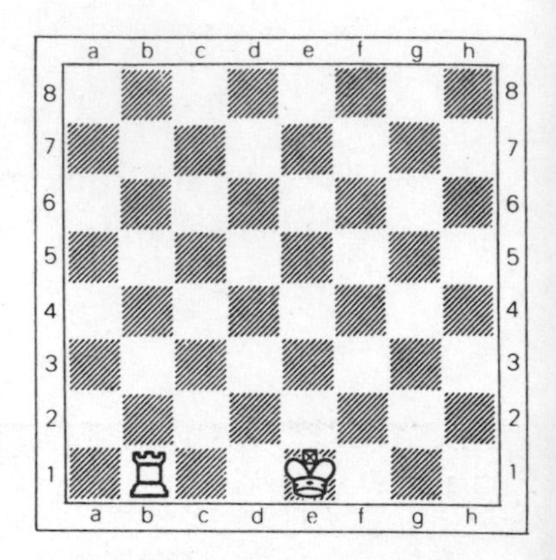

☐ **You cannot castle if you are in check.**

The white king is attacked by the black queen.

White cannot castle to get out of check.

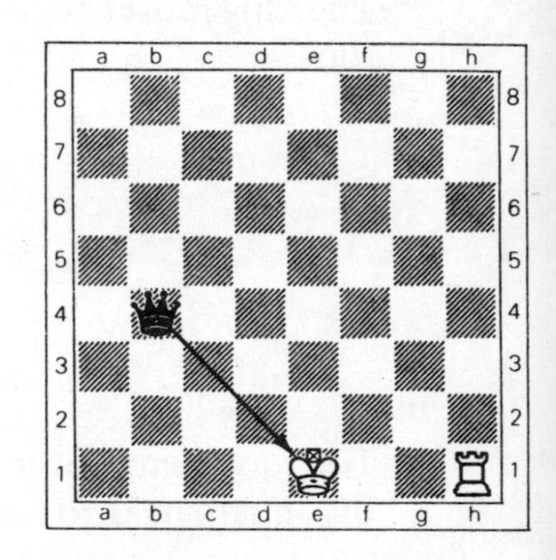

☐ **You cannot castle into check.**

White cannot castle, because his king would move to g1, and on that square he would be in check from the black rook.

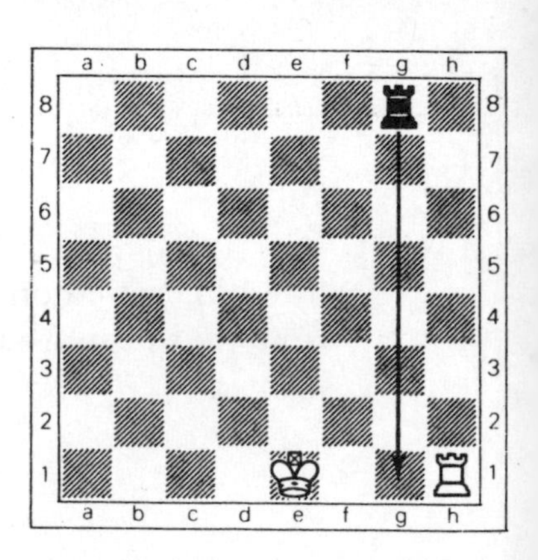

☐ **You cannot castle if your king passes over a square on which he would be in check. You cannot castle 'through check'.**

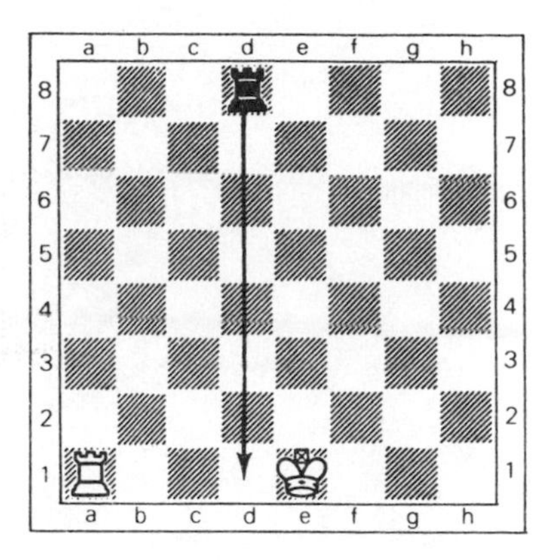

White cannot castle, because to get from e1 to c1 the king has to pass over d1, and that square is attacked by the black rook.

White cannot castle because he would be in check on d1.

☐ **You cannot castle if there is another piece on one of the squares between your king and rook.**

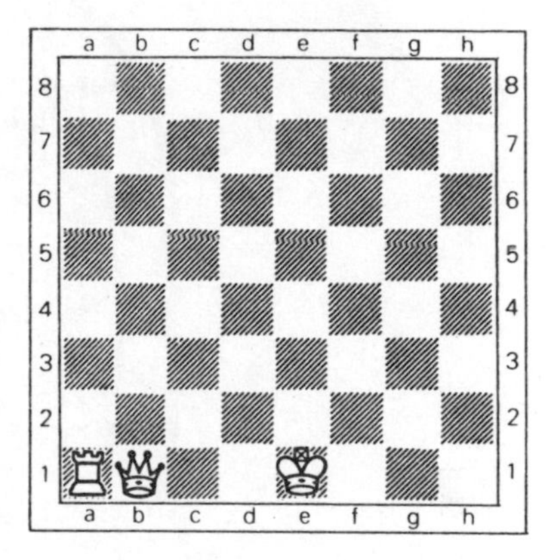

White cannot castle, because his queen on b1 is in the way.

Now you have another move you can add to the game of Mini-Chess.

Play a few games for yourself; see how castling can help you; and get used to the rules.

STEP 10

The Bishop

Almost every army in history has used cavalry, armed soldiers mounted on ponies or horses. The Arabs have even ridden into battle on the backs of camels. But the Indian army went one better; they used elephants! Soldiers stood on a platform built high on the elephant's back, from where they could hurl down missiles upon the heads of any of the enemy foolish enough to come within range. The elephant didn't exactly hurtle into battle, but then it didn't need to. To any foot soldier charging forward, the sight of a troop of elephants lumbering steadily towards him must have been more than a little worrying. At close quarters in pitched battle the elephant must have caused total chaos; the enemy who avoided being speared from above was simply steamrollered down and trampled underfoot! And what could the enemy do to stop the wretched animal? With its thick skin and special armoured protection for its tree-trunk legs there was little, short of a cannon ball, that could stop it! The elephant was a very powerful part of the Indian army, and not surprisingly the Indians named one of their chess pieces the elephant.

The name of the piece changed of course when the game came to this country; not many people in England would have heard of an elephant, let alone seen one! But one thing the people did know about was the Church. The Church in the Middle Ages was very important; it owned almost half the land in the country, and its ministers were among the chief advisers to the king. So the chess piece was named after the most important of the ministers; it was called a *bishop*.

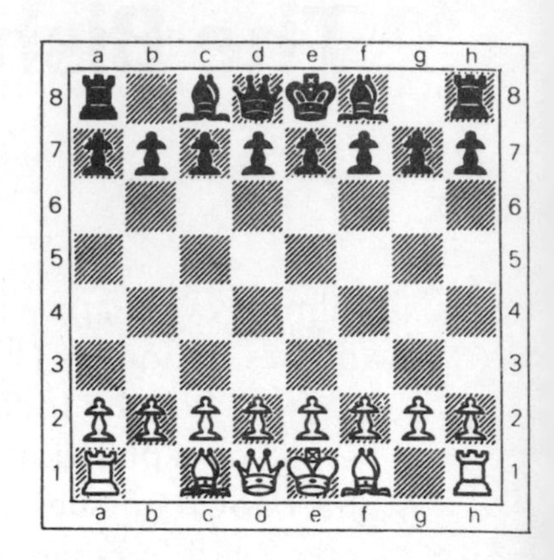

- **Each player has two bishops.**
- **The bishops begin the game either side of the king and queen, the white bishops on c1 and f1, and the black bishops on c8 and f8.**

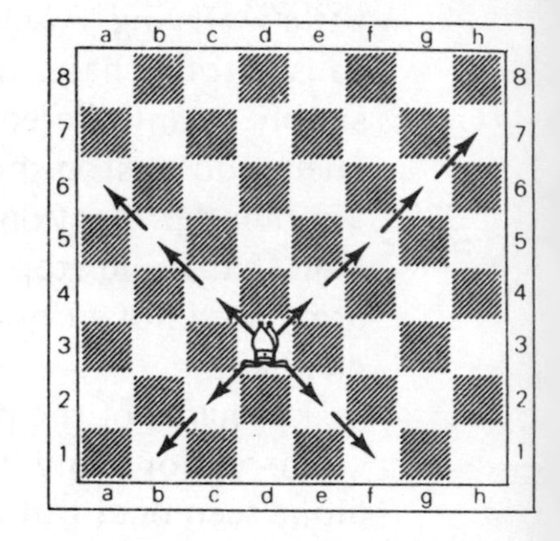

- **The bishop can move in a straight line backwards or forwards along a diagonal.**
- **The bishop can move as many squares as he likes, but he cannot change direction in the middle of a move.**

The bishop on d3 can move to any one of the squares marked with an arrow.

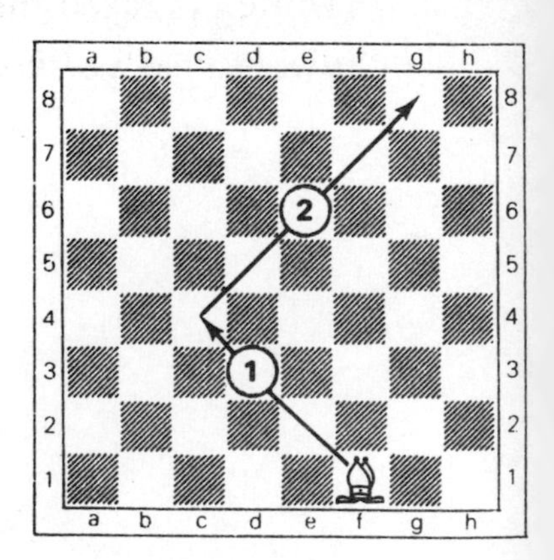

Since it moves only along diagonals a bishop spends all its life upon squares of the same colour.

You have one bishop working on the white squares, and one bishop working on the black squares.

In the diagram you can see a bishop changing direction after one move, but remaining on the same coloured squares.

☐ **The bishop cannot jump over pieces which stand in its way.**

The white bishop can move forward along the diagonal from c1 to e3, but he cannot go to g5 or h6 because he cannot jump over the black pawn on f4.
The white bishop cannot go to a3 because he cannot jump over the white pawn on b2.

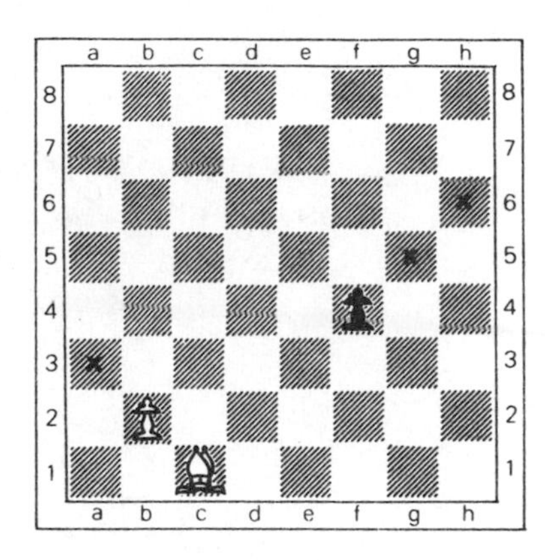

☐ **The bishop captures by making its normal move.**

The white bishop can move from c3 to f6. So the white bishop can capture the black rook standing on f6.

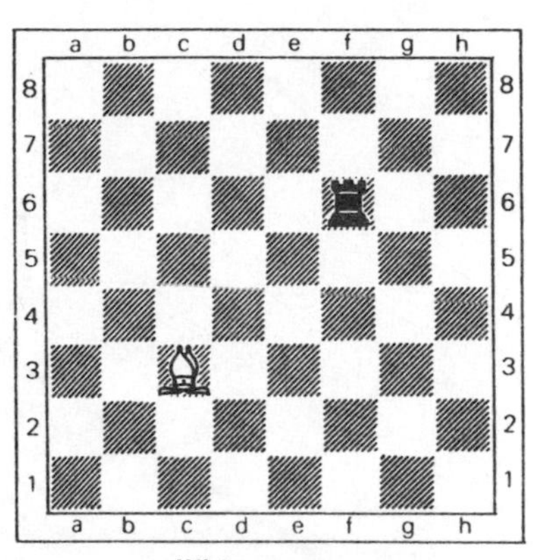

White to move

White has captured.

White has taken the black rook off the board, and moved his bishop from c3 to f6.

(We write this move **Bc3xf6**.)

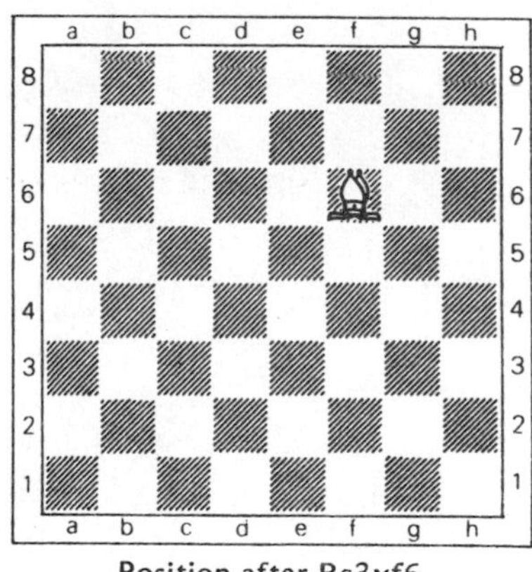

Position after Bc3xf6

Now you only have to learn about one more piece, and you will be playing the real game of chess. Let's get on with it straight away . . .

STEP 11

The Knight

Mounted on a magnificent white charger, polished armour glistening in the sunlight, shield slung low on one arm, lance held high by the other, the noble knight galloped off to rescue the fair maiden in distress, disposing of various dragons on the way. Perched high on a craggy rock the castle loomed up in the distance, drawbridge raised, portcullis firmly in place, and heavily armed men patrolling the battlements. The unfortunate young lady appeared at the uppermost window of the tallest turret, handkerchief waving, ball and chain dragging along behind. The wicked baron rubbed his hands together and grinned evilly down at the lone knight from the gate tower. Five minutes later the baron was dead, two dozen bloodspattered men-at-arms littered the courtyard, several more were hauling themselves out of the moat, and the fair maiden, in a dead faint, was disappearing out through the castle gate on the back of the white charger, requiring only one tender kiss from the lips of the noble knight to bring her back into the land of the living!

A grand fairy tale to flutter the heart of any romantic young girl! Nevertheless, a knight, trained in the art of battle, was a bold and dashing figure at the jousting tournaments, so it is easy to see why one of the chess pieces came to be named after him. Of course in the original game of chess the horse represented the cavalry section of the Indian army. On horseback the rider was able to leap obstacles, ditches, and fences, and in just the same way the chess piece is able to spring about and jump over other pieces which stand in its way.

- ☐ **Each player has two knights.**

- ☐ **The knights begin the game standing between the rooks and the bishops, the white knights on b1 and g1, and the black knights on b8 and g8.**

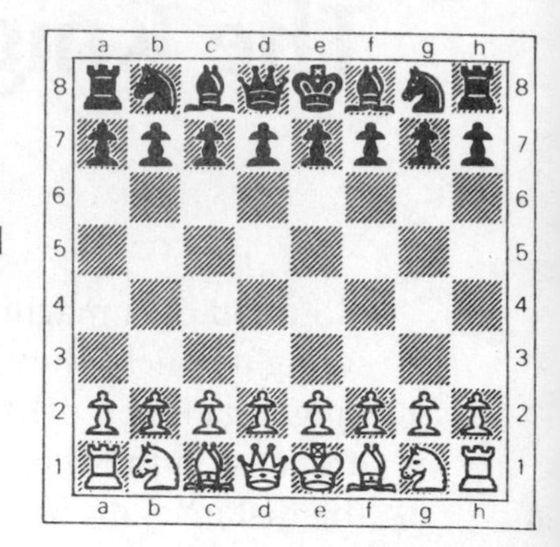

- ☐ **The knight moves two squares along a rank or file, and then turns and moves one square sideways.**

The white knight on g1 has three possible moves.

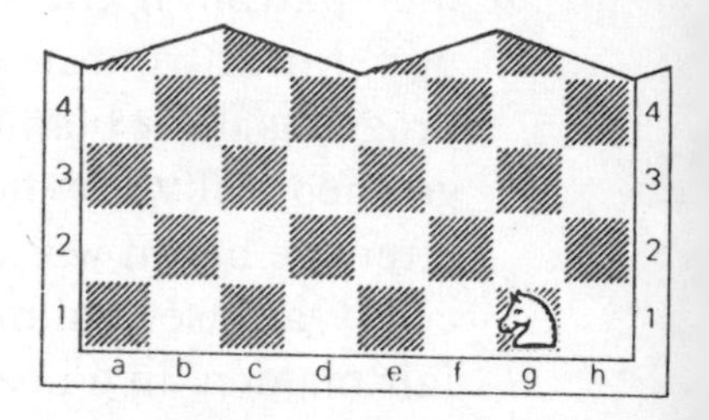

It can move forward two squares along the file and turn one square to the left. (**Ng1-f3**)

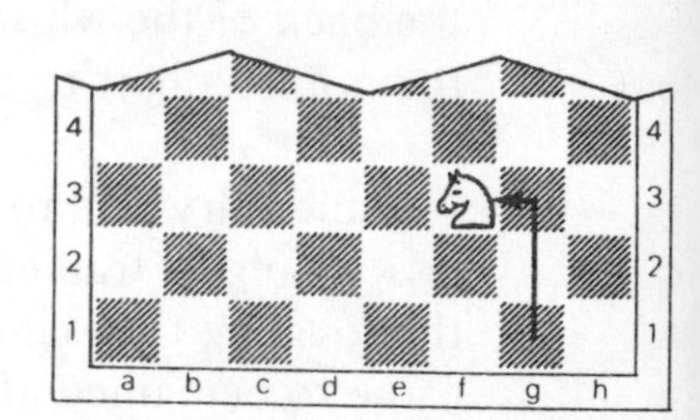

It can move forward two squares along the file and turn one square to the right. (**Ng1-h3**)

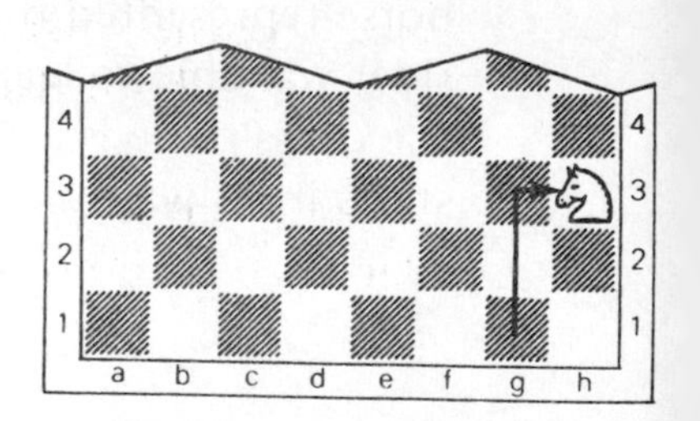

It can move two squares along the rank and turn one square forward. (**Ng1-e2**)

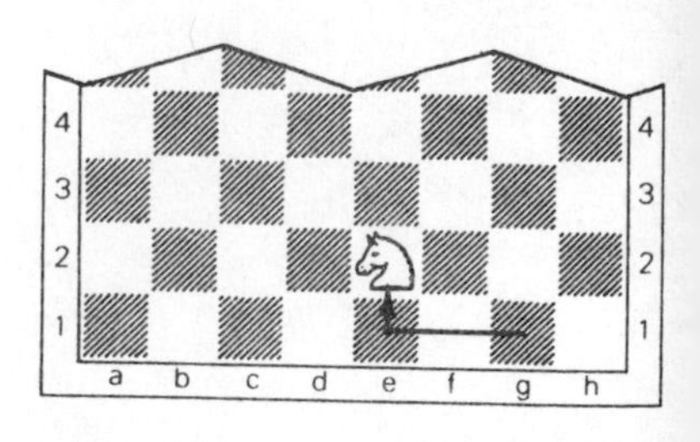

Did you notice how each of the knight moves formed an angle, rather like a capital L?

The knight can move backwards, forwards, and sideways. This white knight, in the middle of the board, can move to eight different squares. We have marked each one with an arrow.

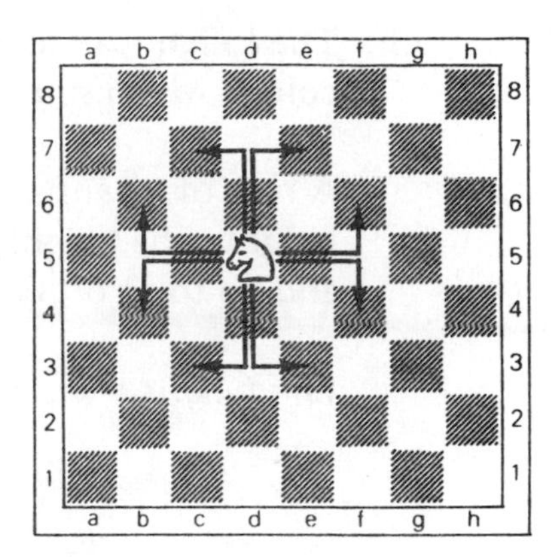

The knight has the most complicated move of all the chess pieces; so we shall do a couple of tests to make sure we have got it right.

1. Put a white knight on f4 on your board. Now, place a pawn on each of the squares to which the knight can move. You should be able to find eight moves.

Look on page 135 and see if you were correct.

2. Now set up your board like this diagram.

You have the knight. You can have six moves running without Black being able to move.

Can you find the way to capture all four black pawns in just six moves?

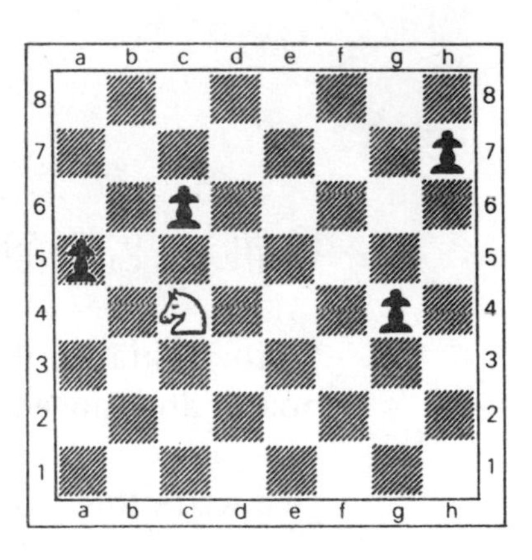

You can set up more positions of your own like this, and see how quickly you can collect all the pawns. The more you practise the sooner you will get used to the way the knight moves.

☐ **The knight can jump over pieces of either colour which stand in its way.**

A row of pawns stands in front of the white knight. The knight may jump over the pawns and go to f3 or h3.

The knight is the only piece that can jump.

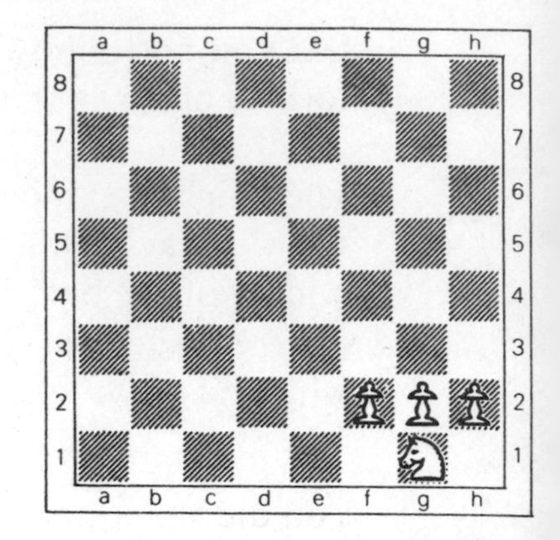

☐ **The knight captures by making its normal move.**

The white knight can move from f3 to e5. So the white knight can capture the black bishop standing on e5.

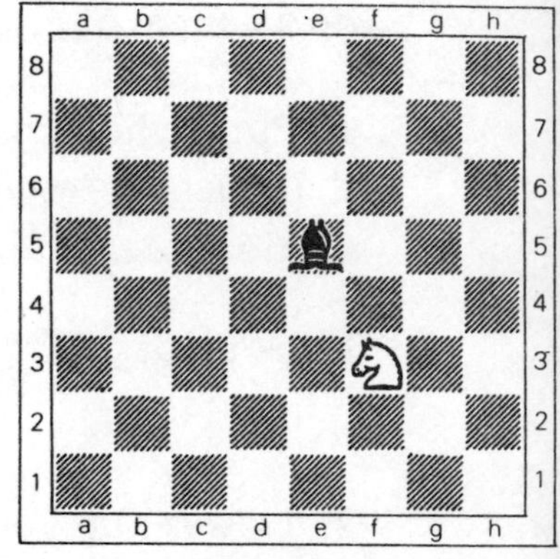
White to move

White has captured.

White has taken the black bishop off the board, and moved his knight from f3 to e5.

(We write this move **Nf3xe5**.)

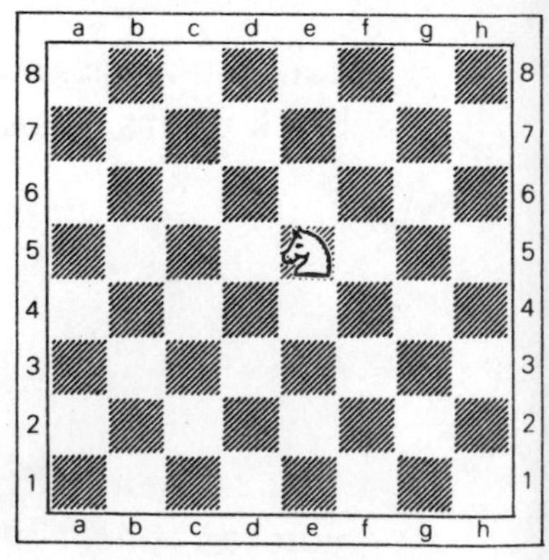
Position after Nf3xe5

Pawn Promotion

When a pawn reaches the far end of the board it is promoted.
The pawn must be removed immediately from the board, and replaced by a queen, a rook, a bishop, or a knight of the same colour.

You did this when you played Queens and Pawns (see p. 28). Then you had to promote the pawn to a queen, but in chess you have a choice. Usually you will choose to turn your pawn into a queen because she is the strongest of the chess pieces, but there may be an occasion when you might prefer to have a rook, a bishop, or a knight. The only piece you may not have is another king!

If you wish to promote a pawn to a queen, and your original queen is still on the board, then there is no reason why you should not have two queens (or three if you get another pawn through!). You will have to borrow a spare queen from another set, or make do by turning a rook upside down.

The Rules

Earl Ulf snorted and let our a roar of laughter. Canute, Viking warrior, King of England, looked puzzled. Ulf grinned at the board and brought his heavy fist crashing down upon the table, slopping ale from his tankard. Upon Canute's face the light was beginning to dawn; the puzzlement turned into anger as he realized he had just placed his knight where it could be taken. Canute had an easy answer to the problem: he simply put his knight back where it had come from and he made another move! Ulf, tankard raised to mouth, spluttered and nearly choked. You could tell he wasn't very pleased; his eyes were wild, his cheeks crimson, and his mouth, dribbling ale into his beard, was twisted in a snarl. Ulf bluntly informed Canute that, King of England or not, he could not take moves back once he had played them on the chess-board. Canute, equally bluntly, picked up the board, broke it over Ulf's head, sending the pieces showering all over the floor, and threw the Earl out of the room.

Canute could not break the rules of chess, and neither can you. There are several rules of play and behaviour at the board, and you must keep to those rules.

☐ **If you touch a piece you must move that piece if you possibly can.**

☐ **If you touch one of your opponent's pieces you must capture that piece if you possibly can.**

☐ **If you want to adjust a piece, to place it properly on its square, then you must tell your opponent before touching the piece.**

☐ **If you place a piece on a square and let go of it, you cannot take the move back. Once you have let go of the piece, the move has been made; you cannot then change your mind.**

☐ **If you castle you must pick up your king first, or the king and the rook together. If you touch the rook first your opponent may make you move just the rook.**

Those are the proper rules of play. They may seem tough, but if you ever play in a match or a tournament you will be expected to stick to them.

Get into good habits of play right from the start. Suppose it is your move in a game. The first thing you do is to think clearly about the position and decide upon the best move you can make. Let us suppose you decide to move your queen from d1 to d7. Before you pick up your queen have one last good look around the board just to make sure that you are not making a mistake, just to make sure you are not putting the queen on a square where she can be taken. Then, when you are sure you haven't missed anything, pick up your queen, move her down the file to d7, put her down, and let go of her.

What you should not do is move her to d7, and then with your hand still touching her, begin to peer all round the board to see if she is safe, and then slide her back a square to d6 and see if she looks any prettier there. You *can* do this—it isn't illegal—you are not breaking the rules. You will have to move your queen somewhere, but you are not forced to move her to d7 or d6 until you have actually let go of her. But don't do this; it is bad manners. Your opponent wants to look at the board, he wants to study the position, he doesn't want to look at your great hand waving about all over the place blocking his view! In any case *you* will also see more clearly if your hand isn't in the way. So:

Think about the position.

Decide the best move.

Check carefully to make sure you are not making a mistake.

Move the piece carefully, put it down, and let go of it.

If you suddenly notice you are making a mistake while the piece is in your hand, simply put the piece back where it came from and start thinking all over again. You will have to move that piece, but at least you will have another chance of finding the best square for it.

If you play sensibly and follow the rules of chess and sportsmanship you will find that better players will take far more notice of you, will be much more impressed by you, and will be much more willing to help you improve. Good manners at the board are as important as good moves.

One thing you should never do at the board is talk. Your opponent wants to think about the game, he wants to study the position, he wants to work out the best move. He doesn't want to listen to your voice rambling on about this, that, and the other. You may gain an advantage by chattering, you may distract your opponent, stop him from concentrating and thinking clearly, you may make him make a mistake. You may even win by putting your opponent off. But . . . what is the point? You are playing chess, and you will get great pleasure from winning, from beating your opponent in a game of skill, from proving yourself the better player. There is little satisfaction in winning if you know you have only won because you talked your opponent out of the game, because you put him off, because you cheated!

You should always be pleasant and polite at the board, but there is never any reason to talk unless you wish to suggest to your opponent that the game be agreed a draw. Sometimes you will reach a position where you can see no way for either player to win; there may be very few pieces left on the board, or the position may be dead even and very dull. In that case you may suggest to your opponent that the game be stopped and called a draw. If he agrees, then a draw is the result, but if he wishes to play on then the game must continue. This is one of five ways that the game may end as a draw.

□ **A game ends as a draw if:**

1. **The two players agree to call it a draw.**

or 2. **A stalemate position occurs.**

or 3. **Both armies are so weak that neither side can force checkmate.**

or 4. **The same position occurs three times during the game.**

or 5. **Fifty consecutive moves are made by each player without a pawn being moved or a capture being made.**

Don't worry too much about these five rules at the moment; you will soon get to understand them as you gain experience by playing.

Finally you must learn to lose in a sporting manner. You will not kick your opponent under the table; nor will you follow Canute's example and smash the board over his head. You will give in gracefully. Before you are checkmated you may decide that there is no point in playing on; you may have lost several pieces; your opponent's army may be far too strong; you know that no matter how well you play you are going to lose. In that case it may be better to give in, to start another game and get revenge. If you want to surrender then you *resign*; you pick up your king and lay him down on his side; this shows that you have given in.

When you lose there are only two things to think about. Firstly ask yourself why you lost. If you can answer that question then you won't make the same mistakes again—or at least not in the next game.

Secondly plan to get your revenge on the chess-board, not by planting a time-bomb under your opponent's queen and quietly leaving the room, but by beating him fair and square next time you play. Losing isn't much fun, and when you lose you should be angry. But you should be angry with yourself, not with your opponent. Canute was angry, but Canute was angry with Earl Ulf. Canute was still angry two days after the game—so angry that he strapped on his sword and set out in search of the Earl. A little later Ulf's head parted company with the rest of his body! And all because Canute didn't know how to lose.

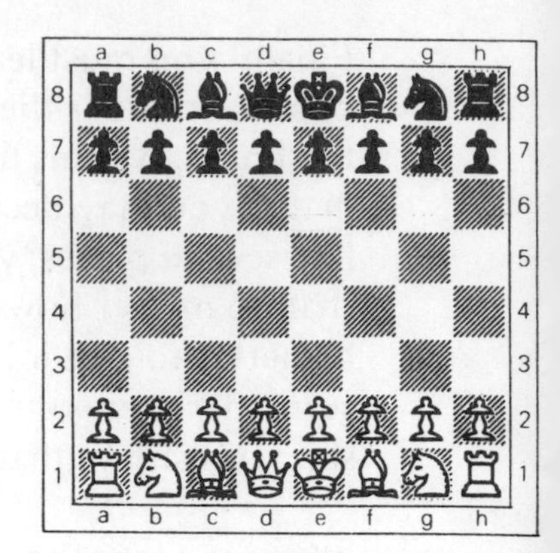

You now know the moves of the pieces and the rules of chess. We will go over them now so that you have a full list to which you may refer:

The board and pieces ready for the start.

A white square in each right-hand corner.

The queens on squares of their own colour.

The aim in chess is to attack the opponent's king in such a way that he cannot escape.
When a king is attacked he is in check.
When a player is in check he must get out of check straight away.
A player has three possible ways of getting out of check:
He can move his king to a safe square.
He can capture the piece that is attacking his king.
He can block the line of attack (unless the attacking piece is a knight).
When a player cannot escape from check he is checkmated, and he has lost.
A player may decide to give up the game by resigning if he can see no point in playing on.

If a player is not in check, yet there is no move he can possibly make, then the position is called stalemate and the result is a draw.
A game can also be drawn if
The players agree to call it a draw.
or Both armies are so weak that neither side can force checkmate.
or The same position occurs three times.
or Fifty consecutive moves are made by both sides without a pawn move or a capture being made.

The king moves one square in any direction.
He captures by making his normal move.

The queen moves any number of squares in a straight line in any direction.
She cannot jump over pieces in her way.
She captures by making her normal move.

The rook moves any number of squares, backwards or forwards, along a rank or file.
He cannot jump over pieces in his way (except during castling).
He captures by making his normal move.

The bishop moves any number of squares, backwards or forwards, along a diagonal.
He cannot jump over pieces in his way.
He captures by making his normal move.

The knight moves two squares along a rank or file and then turns and moves one square sideways.
He can jump over pieces in his way.
He captures by making his normal move.

The pawn moves one square straight forward.
It can move two squares on its first move if it wishes, but even on its first move it cannot jump.
It captures by moving one square diagonally forward.
When it reaches the far end of the board it is promoted to a queen, rook, bishop, or knight.

A player may castle by moving his king two squares towards a rook and jumping his rook over the king to the next square, provided:
Both the king and rook are on their original squares.
and Neither of the pieces has previously moved.
and The king is not in check.
and The king does not pass over a square on which he would be in check.
and The king does not move into check.

Once a player has touched a piece he must move that piece if he possibly can.
If he touches one of his opponent's pieces he must capture that piece if he possibly can.
If he wishes to adjust a piece on its square then he must tell his opponent what he is doing, before he touches the piece.
Once a player takes his hand off a piece he cannot take the move back.

STEP 14

The Values of the Pieces

When you played Pawns you often exchanged a pair of pawns. You took one of your opponent's pawns, he took one of yours; you gained one, you lost one; a fair swap. In chess you will have to make other exchanges, so it is a good idea to know what each of the pieces is worth before you start swapping them off! Obviously you wouldn't exchange your queen for one of your opponent's pawns, you know the queen is far more valuable. But how about exchanging a bishop for a knight, or a rook; would that be a fair swap? Here is a table to show the value of each of the pieces:

Queen	=	9 Points
Rook	=	5 Points
Bishop	=	3 Points
Knight	=	3 Points
Pawn	=	1 Point

This table is only meant as a rough guide to help you when exchanging. You can see that a bishop is roughly equal to a knight, that a bishop and a knight together are worth more than a rook, and so on.

You can also use the table to work out which player has the stronger army at any time during the game. If you add up the points of the pieces you have on the board, and then the points of the pieces your opponent has, then the player with the higher total has the more powerful army. This does not mean that that player is winning. Chess is a battle. Usually battles are won by the stronger army, but not always. You only have to stay awake for a few minutes of a school history lesson to learn that there have been many occasions when a weak army has smashed a strong one!

Dead soldiers aren't much use! Every good general realizes this, and, when he goes into battle, does all he can for the safety of his men—while of course making sure that he wins!

You have to do exactly the same at the chess-board. You want to win. You may be able to throw away several of your pieces and still win, but usually you will do better if you look after your pieces in just the same way a genera looks after his men.

You must look after your pieces.

The white knight has four possible moves. One of them, **Na3-c4**, is bad because on c4 the knight could be taken by the black bishop.

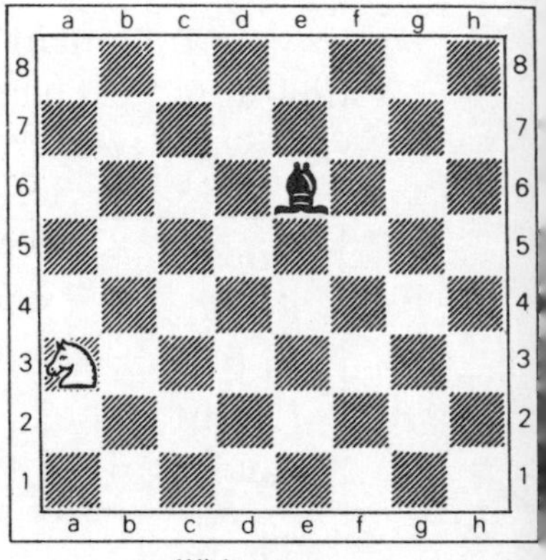

White to move

Now it is safe for the white knight to move to c4.

If the black bishop captures the knight then White will recapture with his own bishop.

White loses his knight and gains a bishop—a fair exchange.

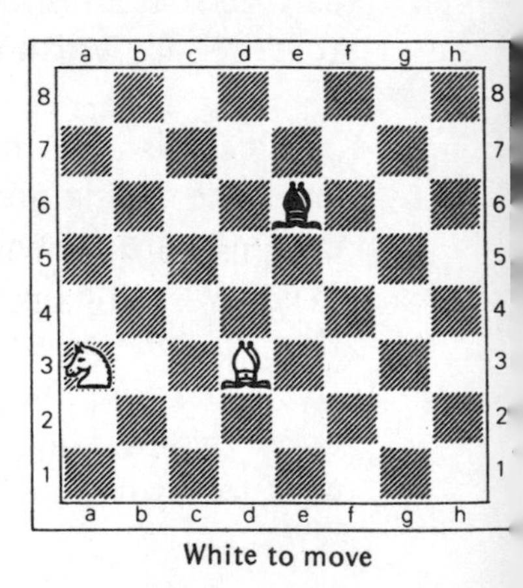

White to move

We can make a simple rule from this. *If you place a piece on a square where it can be taken, you must have as many pieces defending that square as your opponent has attacking it.* If you do not have enough defenders then your opponent will win one of your men.

White has just moved his knight to d4. Is this a safe move?

Well, two black pieces are attacking d4, and two white pieces are defending; so the white knight should be safely defended.

Let's make a few moves and see whether it is.

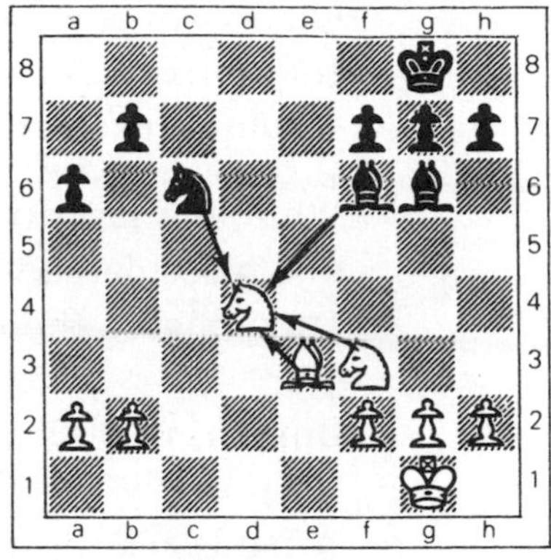

Black to move

Suppose Black captures with his knight:
1 . . . Nc6xd4
And White recaptures with his other knight:
2 Nf3xd4
Black takes with his bishop:
2 . . . Bf6xd4
And White retakes with his bishop:
3 Be3xd4
A fair exchange! White has lost two knights and won a bishop and knight.

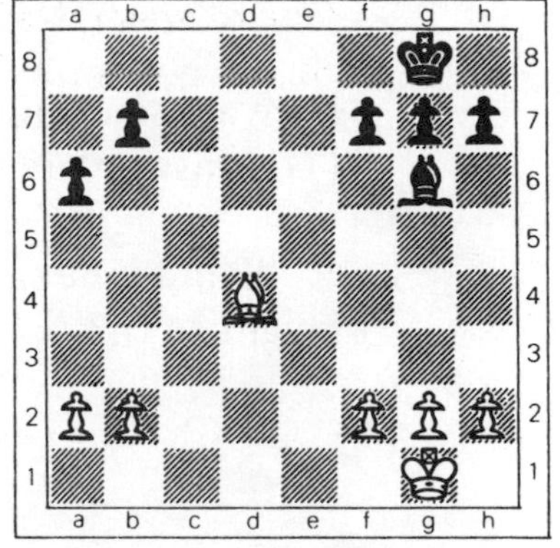

Position after 3 Be3xd4

In this position White has just moved his knight to d5. Is this a safe move?

Well, two black pieces are attacking d5, and how many white pieces are defending?

Only one.

White does not have enough defenders; so Black will win a piece.

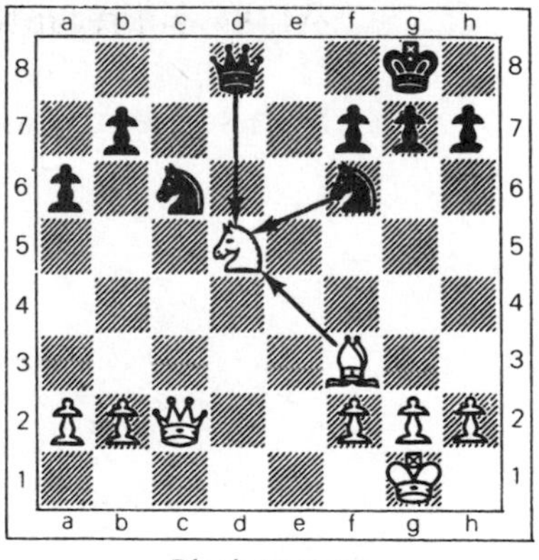

Black to move

Obviously you have to be careful how you use our 'exchanging rule'. A piece for a piece is a fair swap only if the two pieces are the same value. A general wouldn't exchange a tank for a pop-gun, and neither should you!

White has just put his knight on d5. He has one piece defending and black only has one attacking; so the knight should be safe.

But it isn't safe!

When Black captures he will win a knight, but when White recaptures he will only win a pawn.

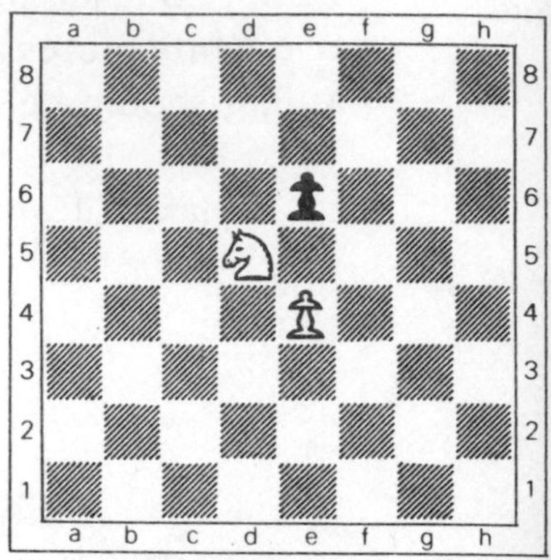
Black to move

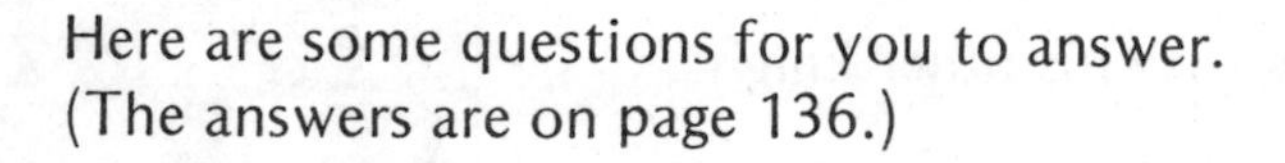
Here are some questions for you to answer. (The answers are on page 136.)

1. Would it be safe for White to move his knight to e4?

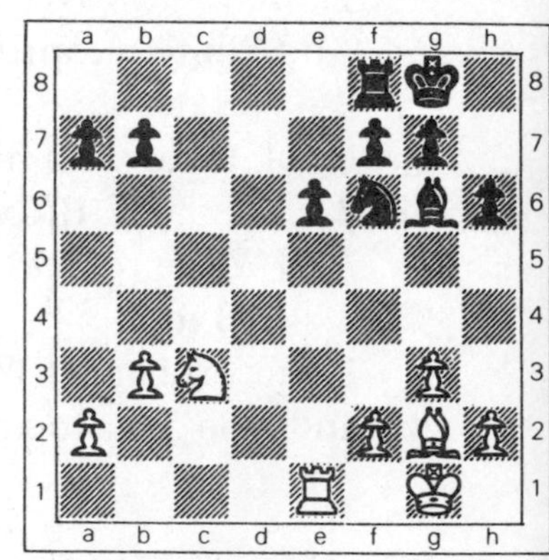
White to move

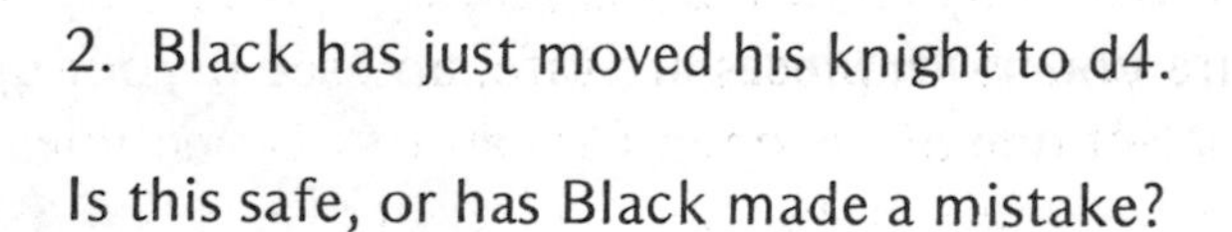
2. Black has just moved his knight to d4.

Is this safe, or has Black made a mistake?

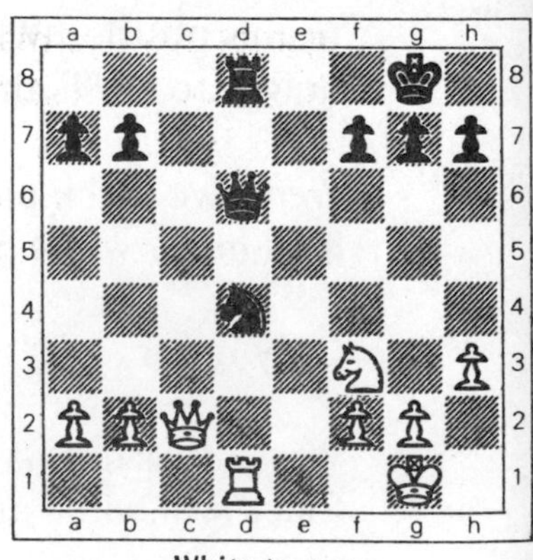
White to move

3. Black has just played . . . **Nf6-d5**.
Is the black knight safe on d5, or is Black going to lose one of his men?

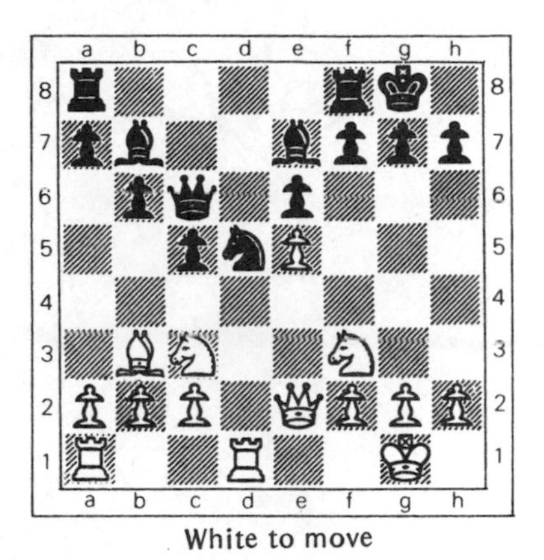

White to move

A game of chess is over when one side has got checkmate. Checkmate is your main aim, but winning pieces can be a tremendous help. In fact to begin with most of your games will be won by your making a large collection of your opponent's pieces, and only then, when your army greatly outnumbers your opponent's, will you turn your attention to attacking and checkmating his king. When you have a lot of pieces and your opponent has only a few, getting checkmate is easy.

Your pieces are gold and you must value them as such. Before every move you must check and recheck to make sure that you are not placing a piece where it can be taken, that you are not leaving undefended a piece which is attacked. Pieces are so important that in a game between the leading players of the world, losing just one single pawn can be enough to cost a player a game! Always make sure your own pieces are safe, and see if your opponent has made a mistake and left one of his open for capture. Sometimes a piece may be just left waiting for you to take, but you must also be on the look-out for little tricks or traps that can win pieces. This is what we shall do next: look at ways which will help you to win pieces.

The Fork

A farmer uses a pitchfork for tossing hay; it is a long wooden pole with two sharp metal points on the end. You can sometimes use a fork to help you win at chess. Not a real pitchfork; sticking the weapon with a mighty thump into your opponent's chest might have the effect of bringing the game to a grinding halt—it might even give you the pleasure of seeing him suffer—but it won't help you win the game! In chess a fork is a double attack. If one of your pieces is attacked you will try to save it, but suppose two of your pieces are attacked at the same time? You only have one move, and you can't save both pieces.

In the diagram one of the white pawns can move forward and attack both of the black pieces.

Can you see which pawn can make this double attack?

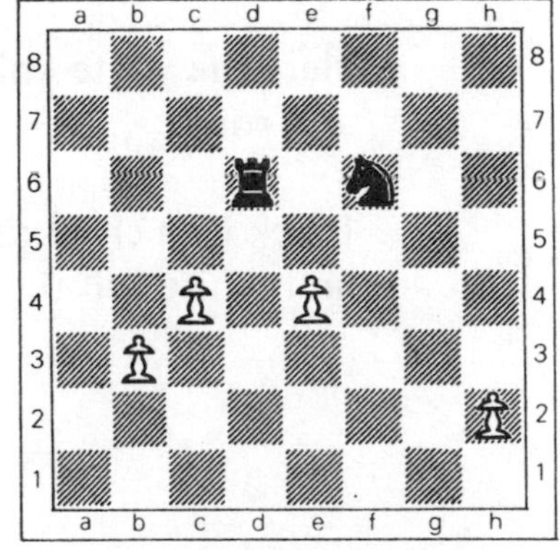

White to move

The white pawn has moved forward from e4 to e5 where it attacks both of the black pieces. The pawn *forks* the black rook and knight. Black cannot save both of his pieces.

If Black saves his rook by moving it, then White will capture the knight with his pawn. If Black saves his knight by moving it, then White will capture the rook with his pawn.

Black must lose one of his pieces because of the pawn fork.

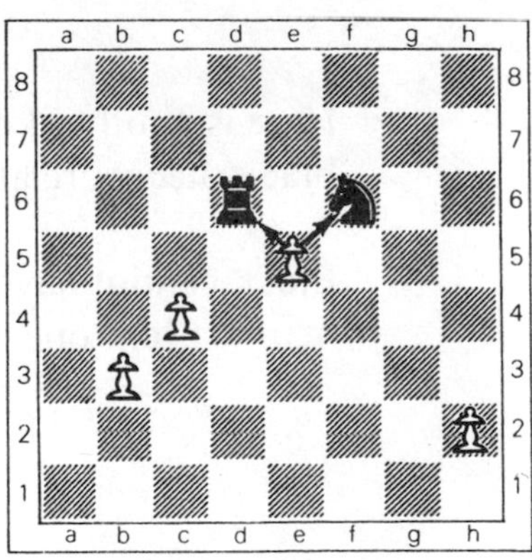

Position after e4-e5

Here is another fork, this time with the black queen. She attacks the white knight and bishop. White must lose one of his pieces.

If he moves his knight he will lose the bishop, and if he moves his bishop he will lose the knight.

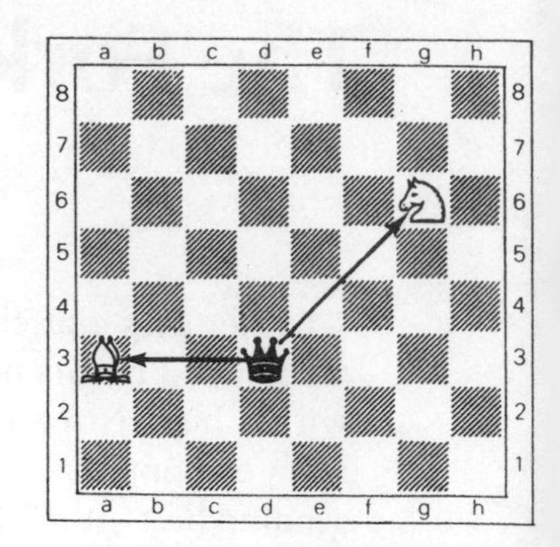

A knight is a very useful piece for forking.

Here the white knight forks the black king and rook.

Black is in check; so he must save his king, and White will then take the rook.

Here is another knight fork; this time three black pieces are attacked.

Black cannot have three moves running, so he must lose one of his men!

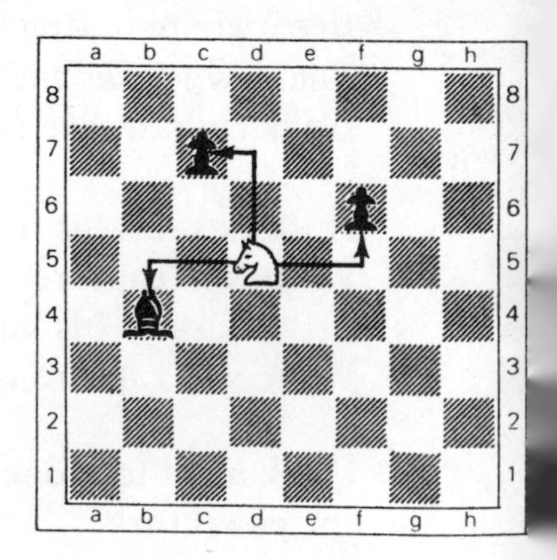

Now for a quiz on forks. You will find answers on page 136.

1. In the diagram you can see a black knight and bishop.

Imagine you have a white rook in your hand. Where could you put that white rook so that it attacks both the knight and the bishop?

There are two places where the rook could be. Can you see them both?

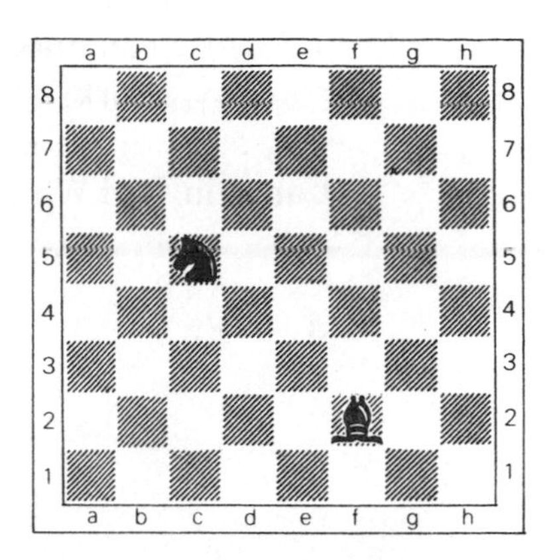

2. This time you have a black knight. Where could you put that knight so that it forks the white king and queen?

There is only one square from which the knight will attack both white pieces.

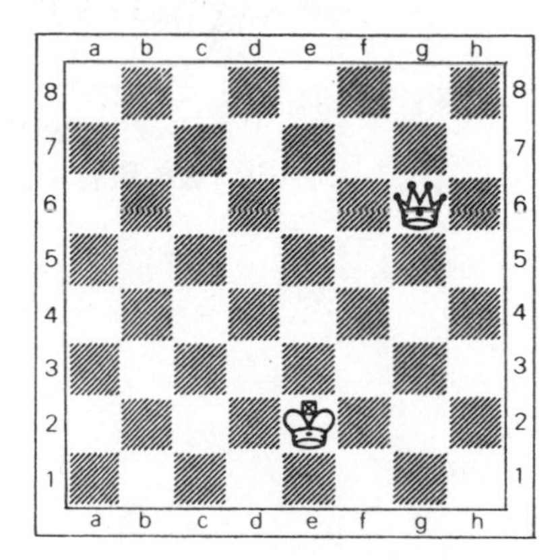

3. Where could you put a white bishop so that it forks the black rook and knight?

There are two different squares from which the bishop will attack both black pieces.

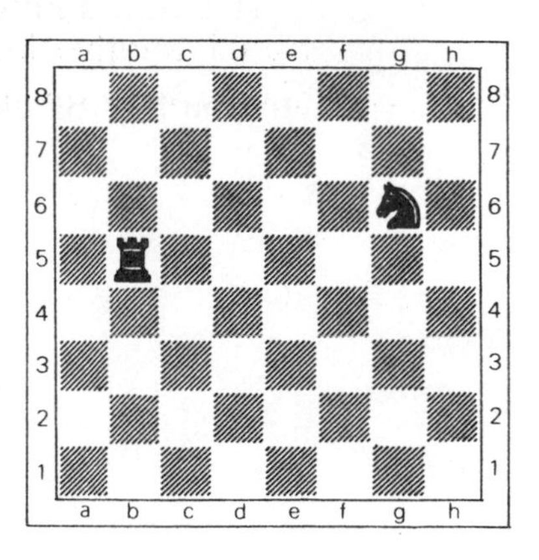

Here are six more forks for you to find. The answers are on p. 136.

1. White can make a capture and win a black rook by a fork.

Can you find White's move?

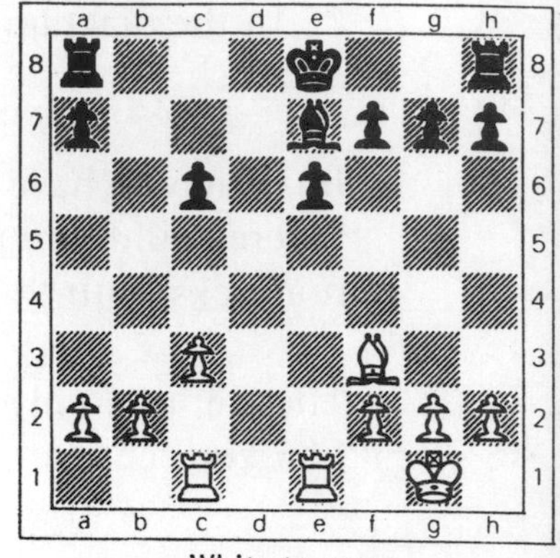

White to move

2. Another bishop fork.

Can you see how White's bishop can move to attack two black pieces?

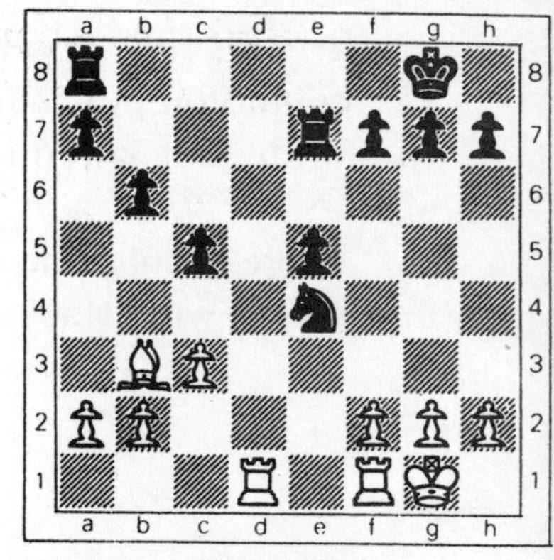

White to move

3. This time a knight fork.

Can you find Black's move?

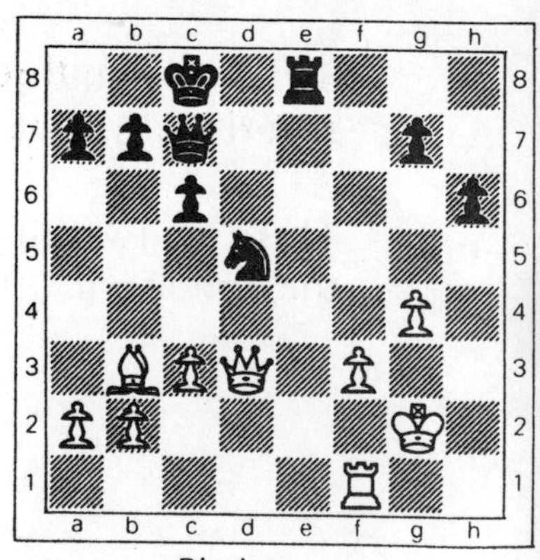

Black to move

4. Black is threatening to win at once. If he plays . . . **Qh5xd1** it is checkmate!

White could save himself by moving his rook, but can you find a better move for White?

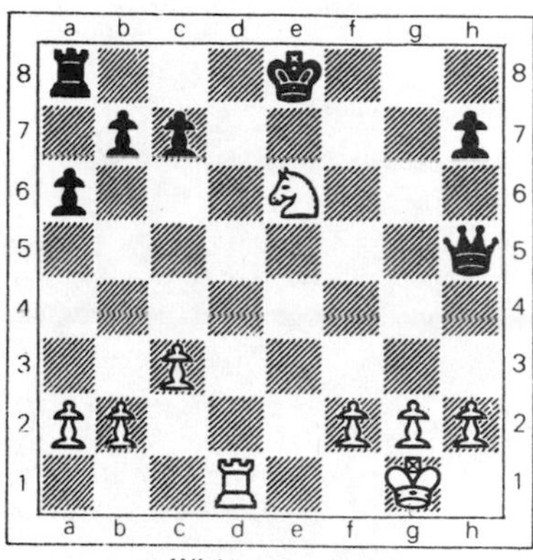
White to move

5. Black has two possible forks in this position; one is good, one is bad.

What move would you play for Black?

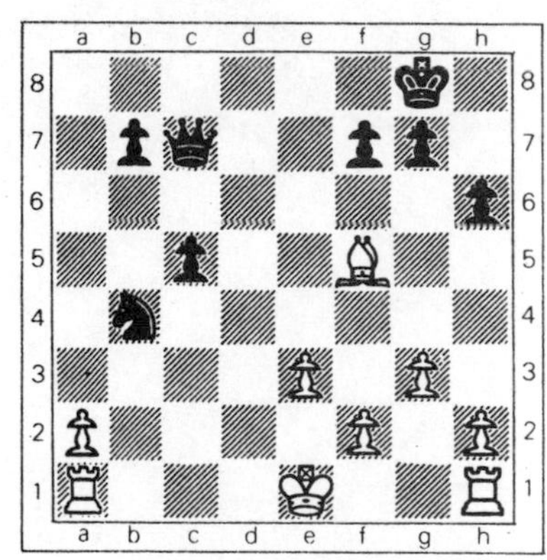
Black to move

6. A fork here threatens checkmate. Can you find White's move?

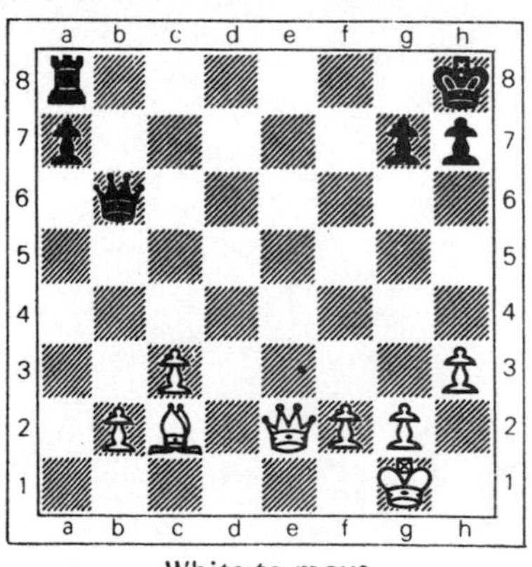
White to move

The Pin

You use a pin, like a nail, for fixing two things together. In chess a pin is a method by which you nail two enemy pieces together on the same line. You attack one of the pieces, and if it moves away to save itself then the second piece on that line is left open for capture. If you look at the diagram below you will see what we mean.

The two black pieces are on the same file.

The black knight is attacked.
Black cannot save his knight by moving it because his king would be in check.

The black knight is *pinned* to the king.

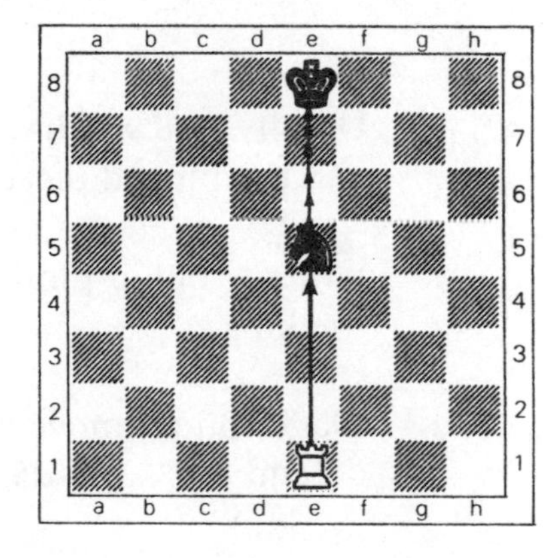

The two white pieces are on the same diagonal.

The white knight is attacked.
If White moves his knight then he opens the diagonal and leaves his queen to be captured.

The white knight is *pinned* to the queen.

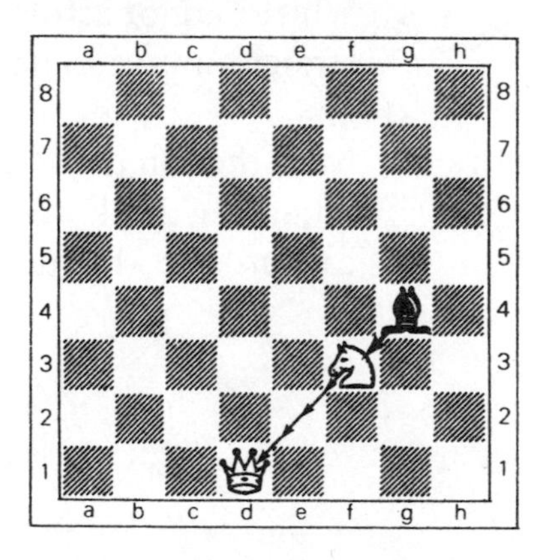

Whenever a piece is pinned you should be on the look-out for a way to win that piece. Sometimes the pinned piece will just fall into your hands like an over-ripe apple from a tree.

White's bishop is pinning the black knight to the rook.

If Black moves his knight, then his rook is captured.

There is no way Black can defend his knight; so he must lose a piece.

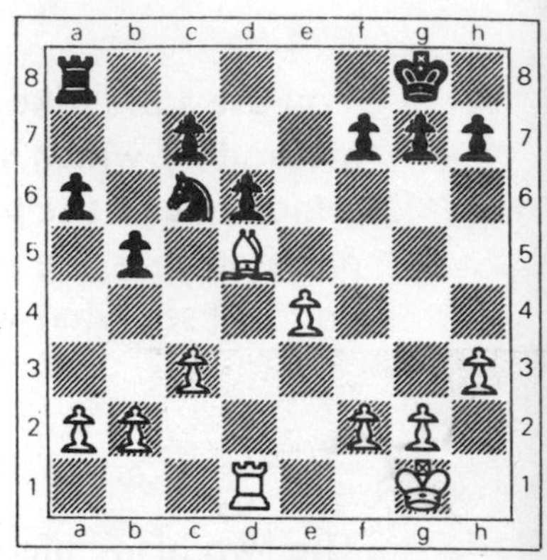
Black to move

Usually you will have to work a bit harder to win the pinned piece!

White's rook is pinning the black knight to the king.

Black cannot move his knight, so he must defend it: . . . **d6-d5**.

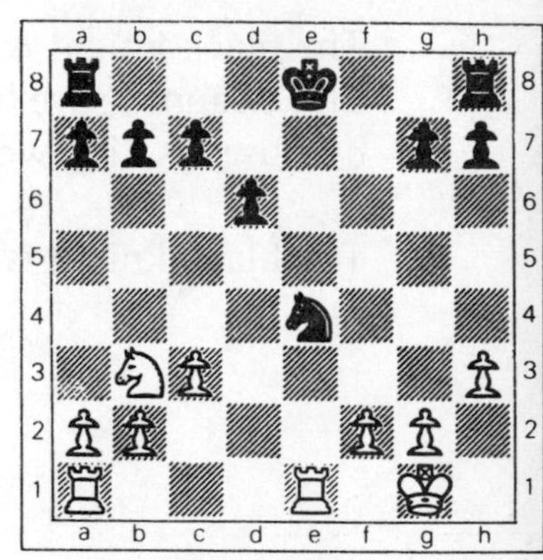
Black to move

White cannot afford to take the black knight straight away; so he attacks it again: **f2-f3**.

Now the pin is going to cost Black his piece. Whatever Black does, White will be able to capture the knight with his pawn.

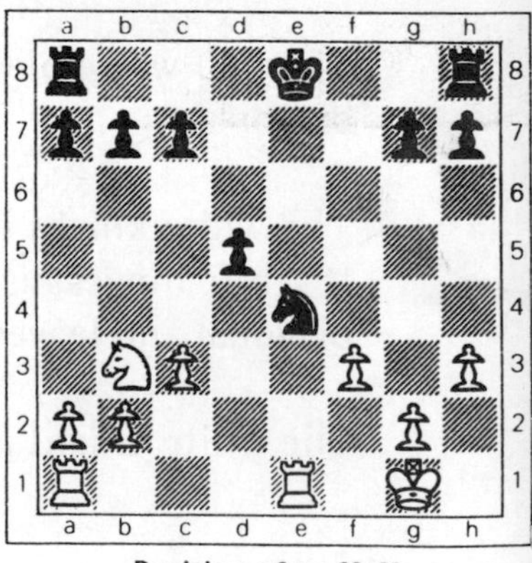
Position after f2-f3

Question time again! You will find the answers on page 136.

1. Black's king and queen are on the same diagonal.

Can White take advantage of this with a pin?

Can you find the move White should make with his bishop?

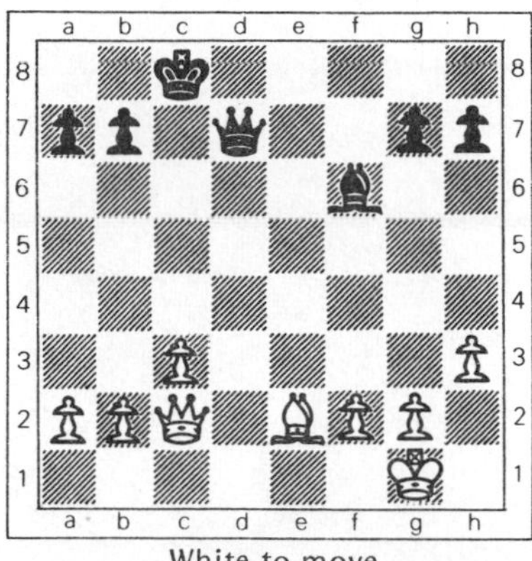

White to move

2. White's knight is pinned to his queen.

How can Black take advantage of this and win the knight?

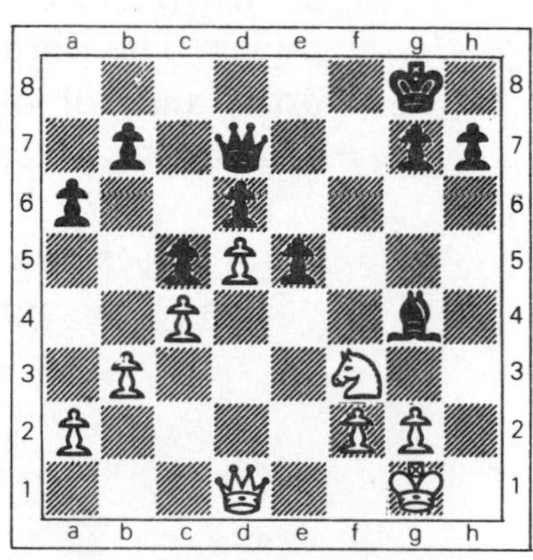

Black to move

3. Black can capture the white pawn on e4 with his queen.

Is it safe for Black to make this capture, or does White have a deadly reply ready?

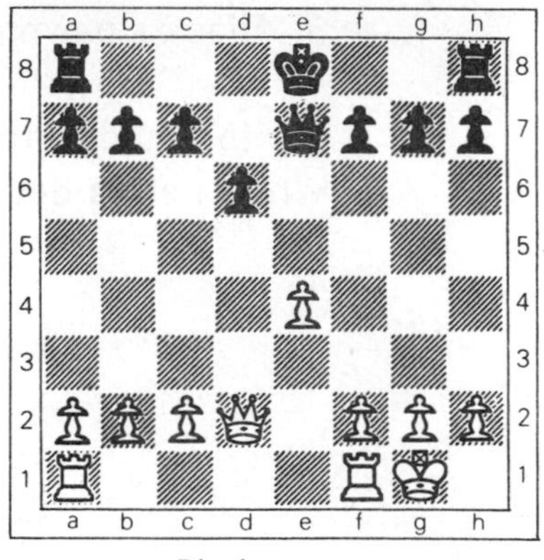

Black to move

4. Can you find a winning pin for White in this position?

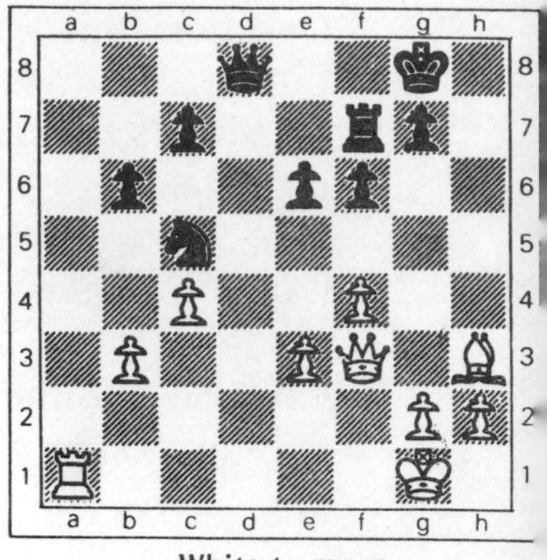

White to move

5. When a piece is pinned it loses a lot of its power. The white pawn on f2 should be doing a useful job defending the bishop on g3. But the white pawn is pinned to its king.

Can you see how Black can take advantage of this to win a piece?

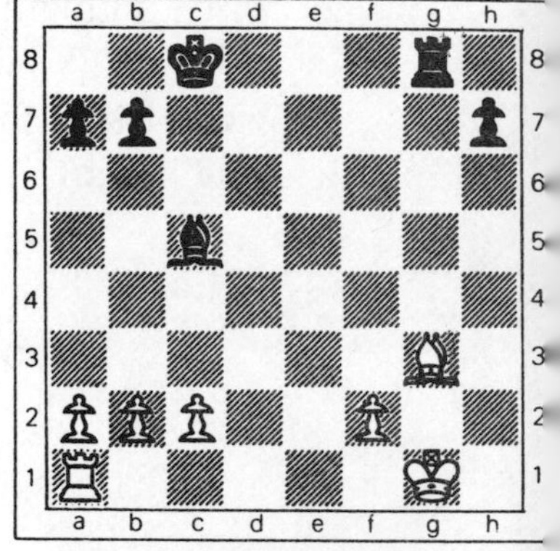

Black to move

6. Black's pawn on d5 is pinned.

White could simply take this pawn, but does White have a better move?

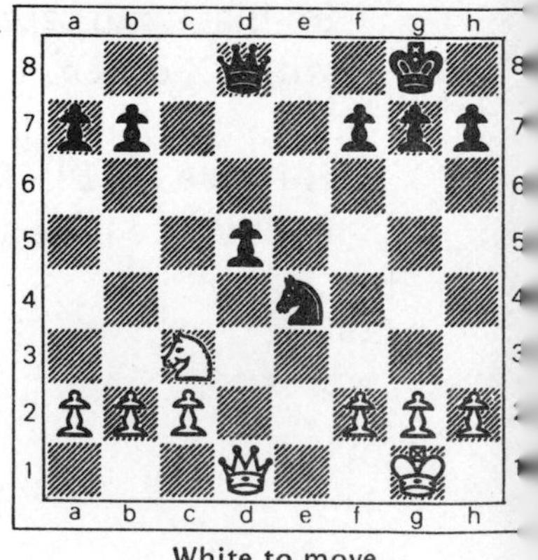

White to move

A different kind of pin is a *skewer*. Again two enemy pieces are nailed together on the same line. This time you attack one piece, forcing it to move, which leaves the second piece open for capture.

Black is in check along the rank.

He must move his king to escape, and then his queen can be taken.

Black's king and queen are *skewered.*

Now another quiz; answers on page 136.

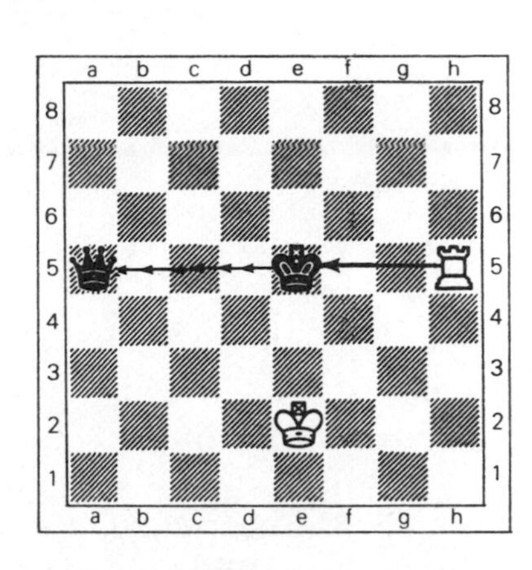

1. Can you find a skewer for White in this position?

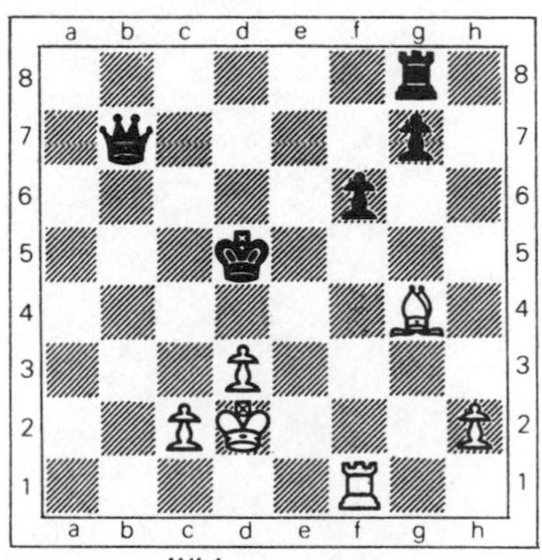

White to move

2. Black threatens to play . . . **Qe5-a1 mate**. White can save himself by means of a skewer. Can you find White's move?

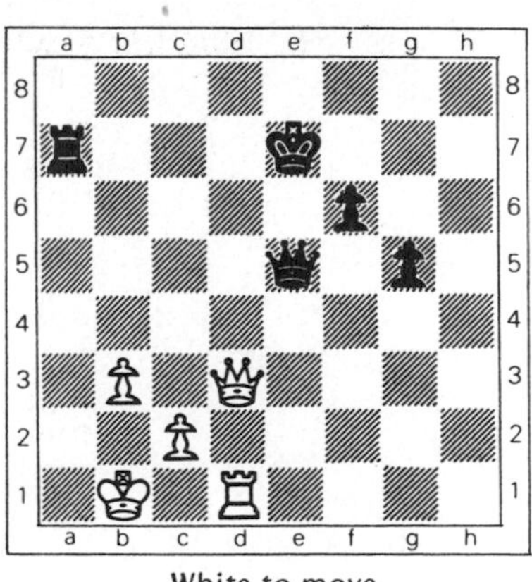

White to move

STEP **17**

The Discovered Attack

Sometimes an attack on a piece can be hidden. You and your opponent both have a piece on the same line, you cannot take his piece because another of your own men stands in the way. But, if you move this other man then you uncover the attack. This will be clearer if we look at an example:
The black bishop on c8 has a hidden attack on the white queen.

If Black moves his pawn from d7 then the queen will be attacked.

White will then have to spend his next move saving his queen.

Black moves his pawn to d5.

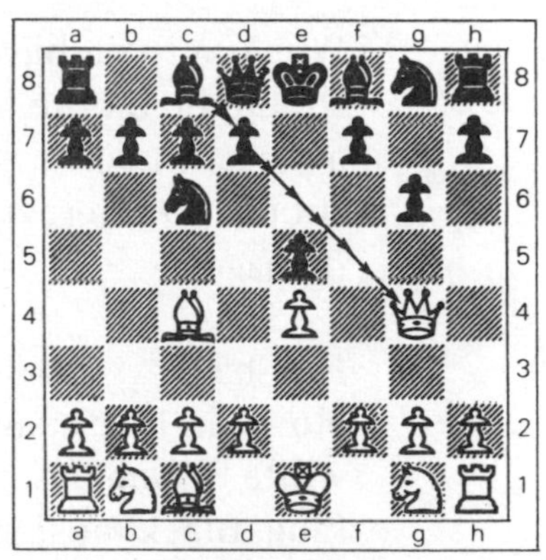

Black to move

Two white pieces are attacked.

Black's bishop has a *discovered attack* on the white queen.

Black's pawn attacks the white bishop.

White will save his valuable queen, but he must lose his bishop.

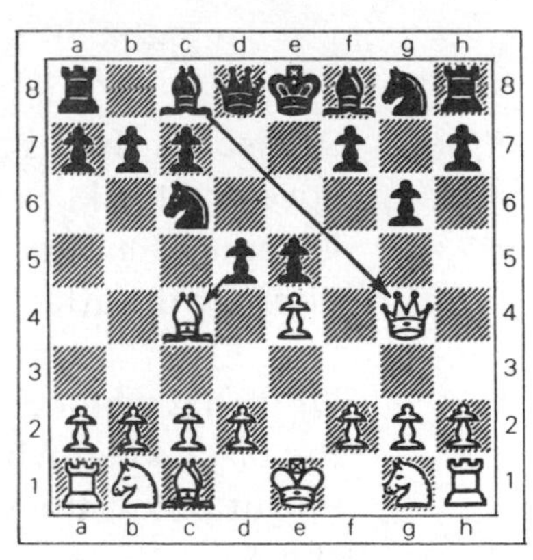

Position after . . . d7-d5

Black was able to use his discovered attack to win a piece.

Here is another example.

White's rook has a hidden attack upon Black's queen. All White has to do is move his bishop out of the way and the black queen will be attacked. But where should the white bishop go? There are several squares, but which one is best?

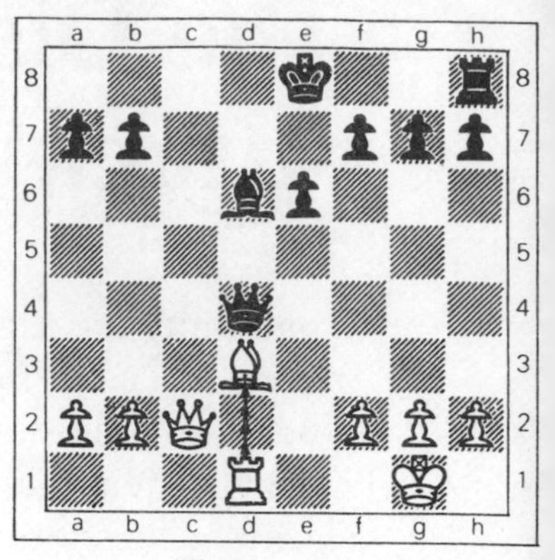
White to move

Whenever you have a hidden attack you should be on the look-out for a way to win a piece. In our position the white bishop should go wherever it causes the most damage!

Bd3-b5+
How can Black save his queen? He can't! The white bishop has moved to attack Black's king. Black must spend his next move getting out of check, so he can't save his queen.

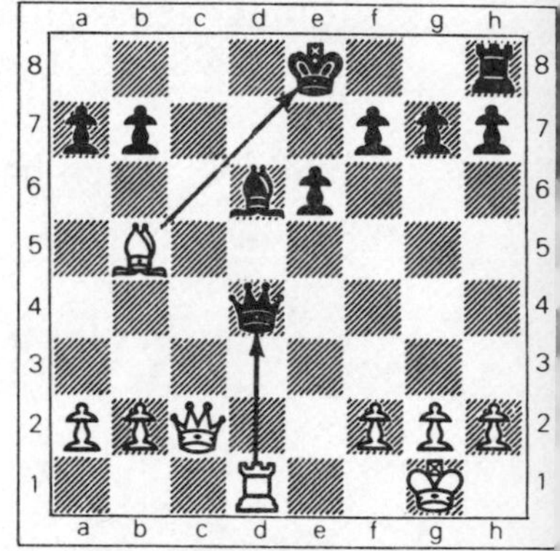
Position after Bd3-b5+

A check is always a useful move in a discovered attack. Sometimes the hidden attack is upon your opponent's king; then when you discover the attack you are *discovering check*.

White has a hidden attack with his rook on the black king. White only has to move his knight out of the way and Black will be in check.
Question: Where should the knight go?
Answer: Where it causes most damage!

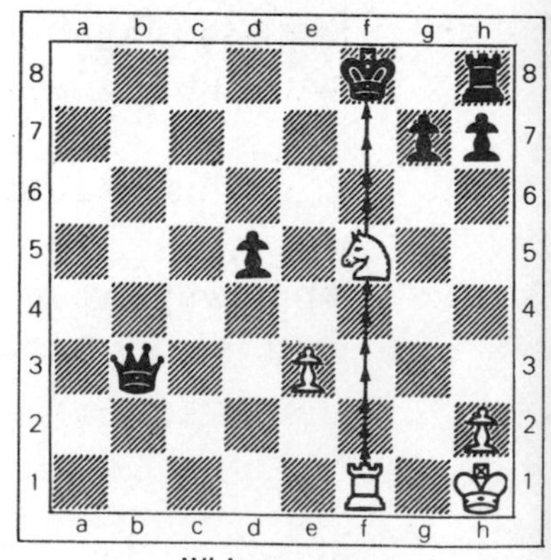
White to move

Nf5-d4+
The white knight has done its damage! With his knight move White has discovered check and also attacked Black's queen.

The important point is that when you discover check your opponent has to get out of check immediately.

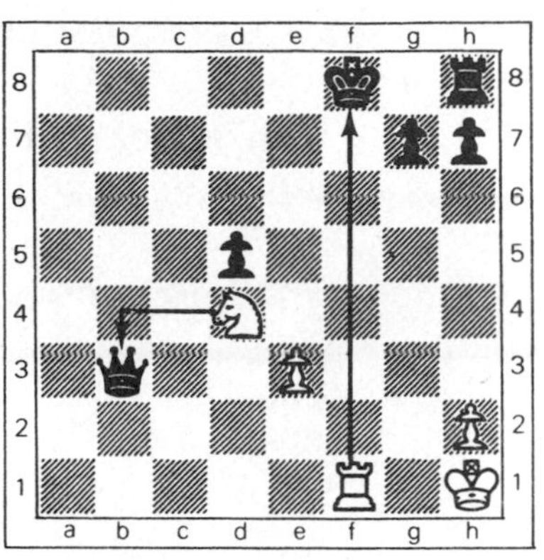

Position after Nf5-d4+

Sometimes you can afford to be 'brave' with the piece you are moving:

White has a hidden attack with his queen on the black king. White only has to move his knight out of the way and Black will be in check.

But where should the knight go to cause the most damage?

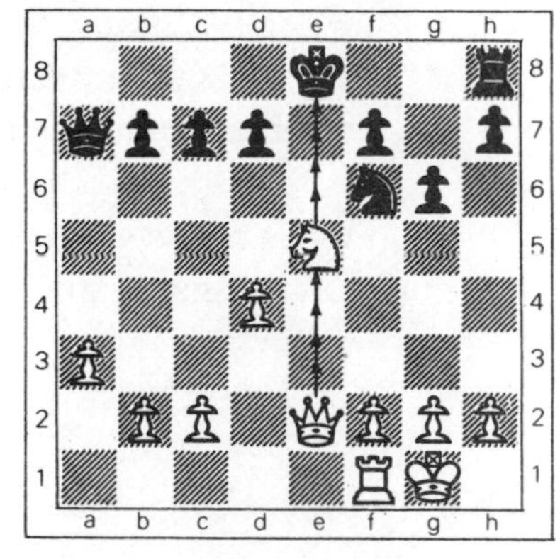

White to move

Ne5-c6+
Normally this move would be a dreadful mistake, because one of the black pawns would capture the knight. But Black is in check. He won't have time to take the white knight. The discovered check allows White to be 'brave' with his knight; it allows him to put it on a square where it could normally be taken.

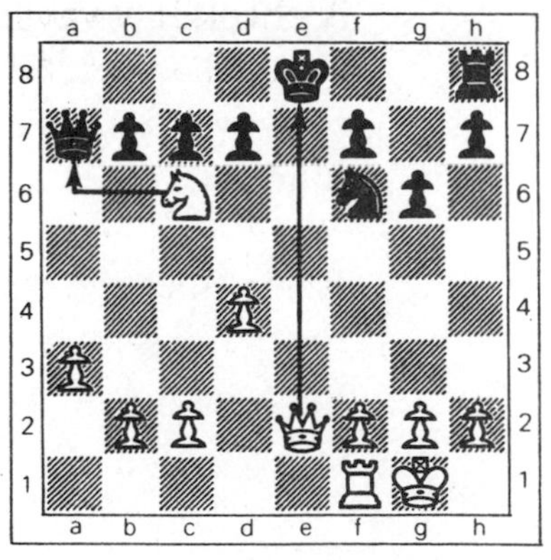

Position after Ne5-c6+

Six more questions for you (answers on page 136):

1. White has a discovered check which will allow him to win the black rook.

What move should White play?

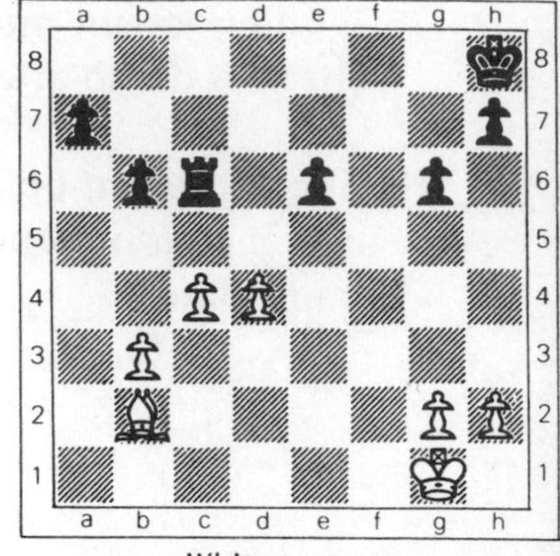

White to move

2. The white bishop has a hidden attack on the black queen.

What move should White play to take advantage of this?

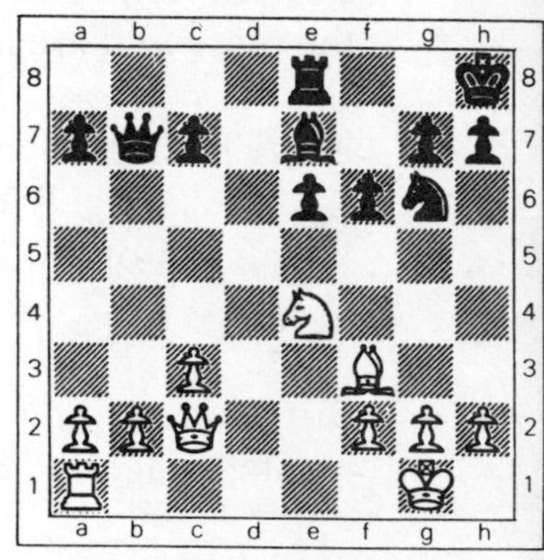

White to move

3. Black is in check.

How would you get out of check if you were Black?

Remember the discovered attack!

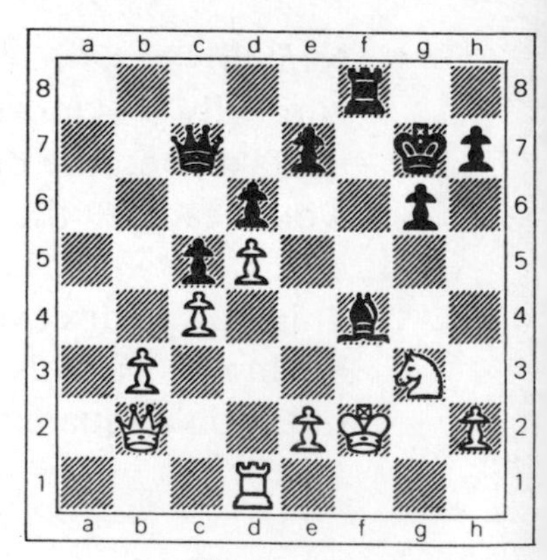

Black to move

4. White has a hidden attack on Black's queen.

Do you see how White can win the queen?

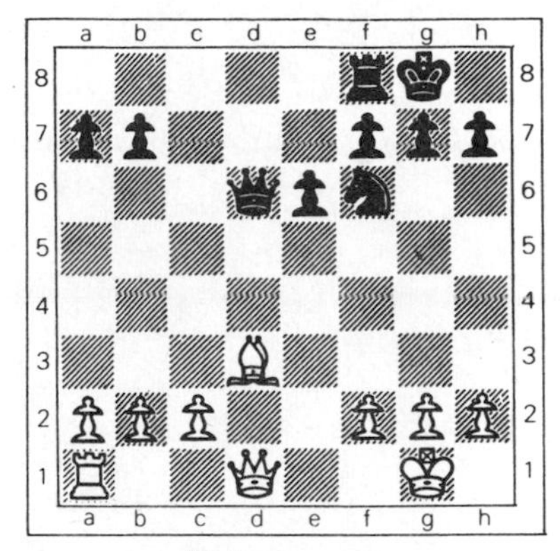

White to move

5. Black can win the white queen by . . . **Rg2-c2** discovering check, but can you find an even better way of discovering check?

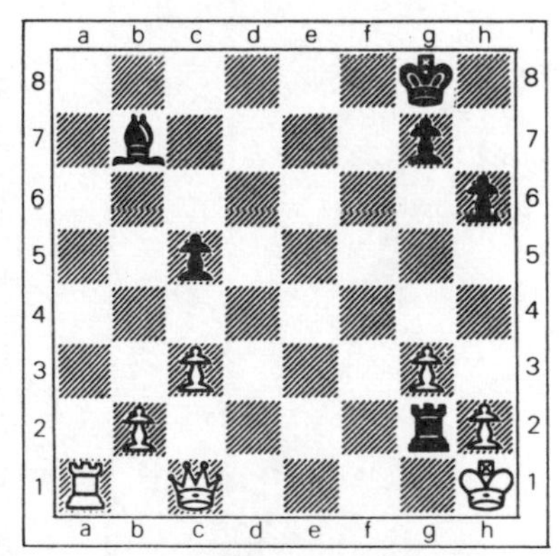

Black to move

6. White can win a piece by **Be2xh5**. Is it safe for White to make this capture?

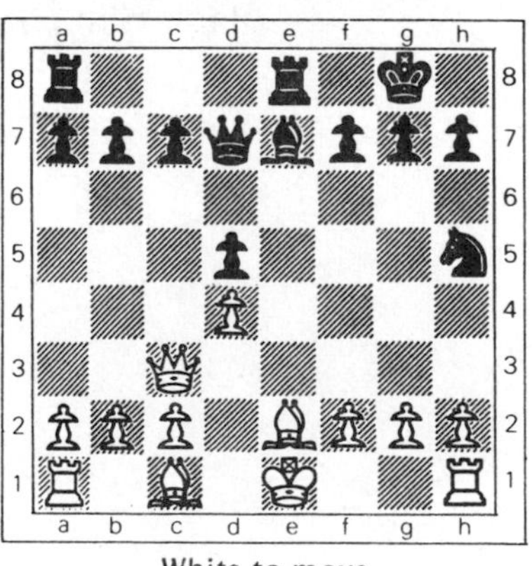

White to move

STEP 18

Destroying the Defender

Have you ever stood on the top rung of a ladder and wondered what would happen if some kind friend came along and kicked the bottom away?! Chess pieces find themselves in this position sometimes.

The black queen seems happy enough; she's attacked by White's queen, but defended by a knight.

White kicks the ladder out from underneath her.

White captures the black knight:

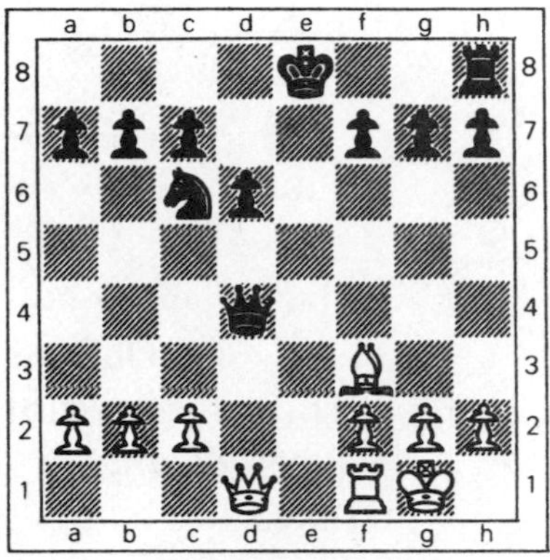

White to move

Bf3xc6+
Now the defending knight has been destroyed, and what is more Black has to get out of check. Black's best reply is to take the bishop:

. . .   **b7xc6**

But now the black queen is left high and dry without a defender in sight, and White's queen will capture her next move.

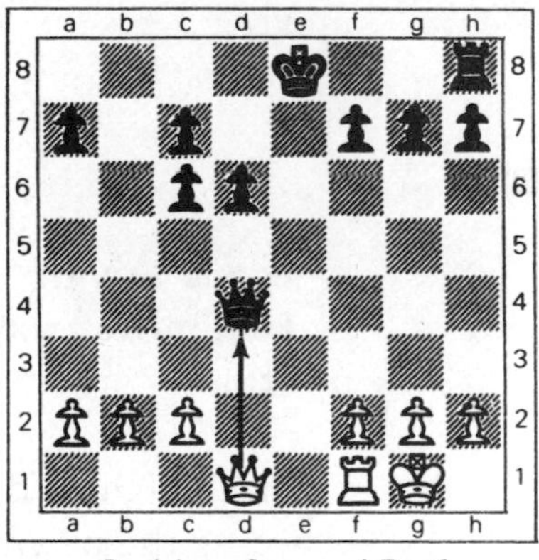

Position after . . . b7xc6

Often pieces appear to be defended when in fact they are not. Here the black queen looked safe, but she wasn't, simply because her defender could be destroyed. You should always be on the look-out for a chance to win a piece by putting an enemy defender out of action.

There are three ways in which we can 'destroy' a defender. The one that we have already looked at is simply to capture the defender. Here is another example:

White's queen is doing a defensive job; she is guarding the bishop.

Black destroys the defender by capturing the queen.

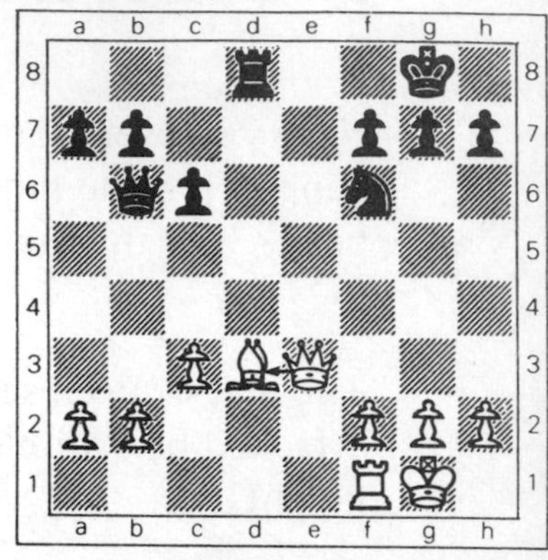

Black to move

Black plays:

. . . **Qb6xe3**

White must recapture or else he will be a queen down:

f2xe3

And now the white bishop is left unprotected and Black's rook will pounce next move.

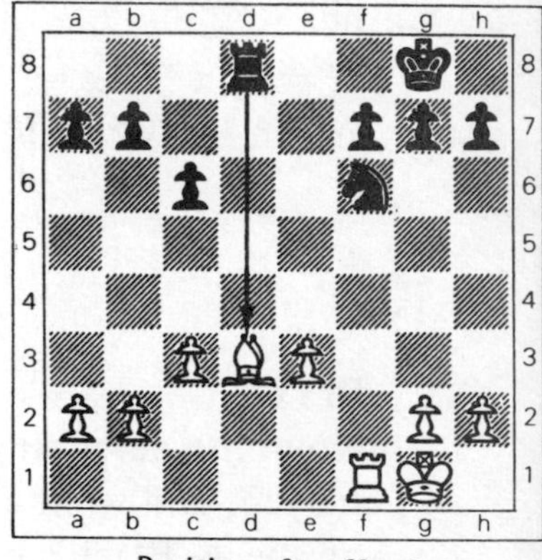

Position after f2xe3

A second way of 'destroying' a defender is to make it move away from its defensive position.

Black's knight is doing a defensive job; it is guarding the pawn on d5.

White destroys the defender by making him move.

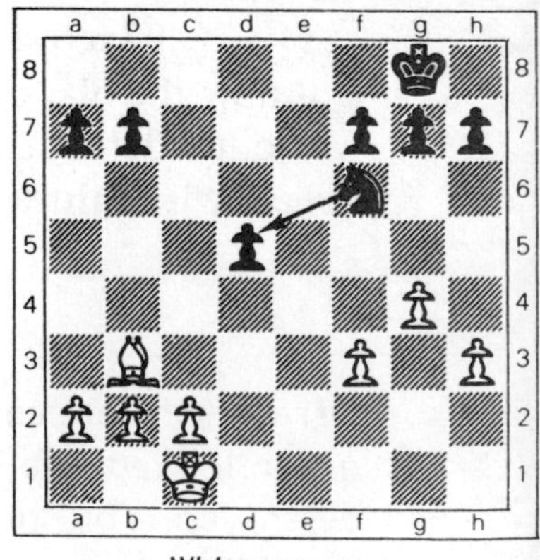

White to move

White attacks the black knight with a pawn:
g4-g5
Black has two men attacked, and he must lose one of them. If he doesn't move his knight it will be taken, and if he does move the knight White's bishop is waiting to gobble up the pawn on d5.

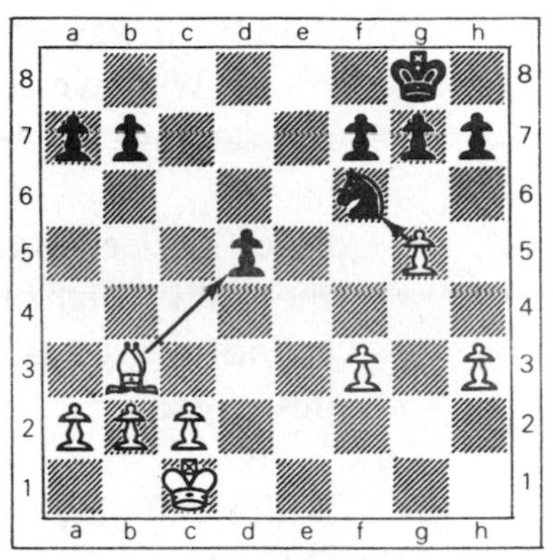

Position after g4-g5

In the next example Black's queen is overloaded with work.

The black queen is doing two defensive jobs; she is defending both the knight and the bishop.

White destroys the defender by making her move.

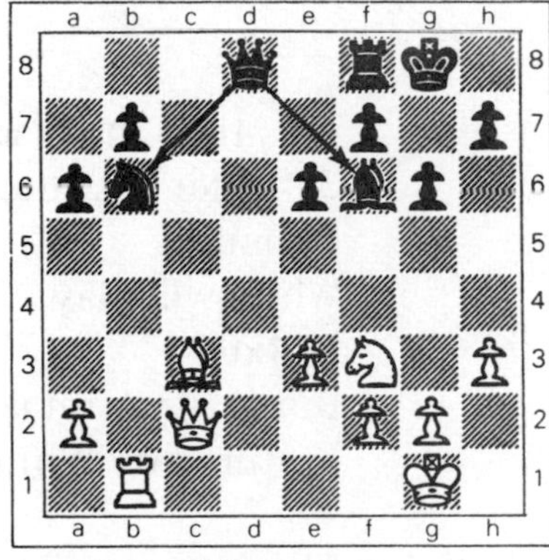

White to move

White plays:
Bc3xf6
Black has lost a piece.
If he recaptures, then his queen must leave the knight undefended, and White's rook will sail merrily down the file and capture the black horseman!

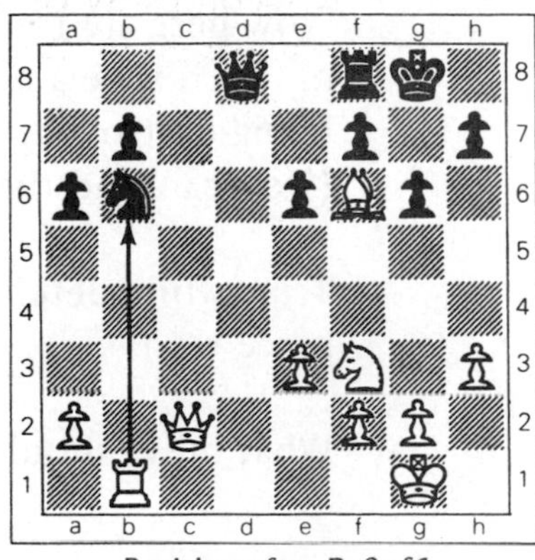

Position after Bc3xf6

The third way of 'destroying' a defender is to tie it down so that it cannot move. We have already seen one example of this when we looked at *The Pin* on page 87, but it won't hurt to study another couple of examples.

Black's queen is defended by the knight. But the black knight is pinned against its king; it cannot move; its defensive powers have been destroyed.

White will play:
Qd1xd4
And Black cannot retake.

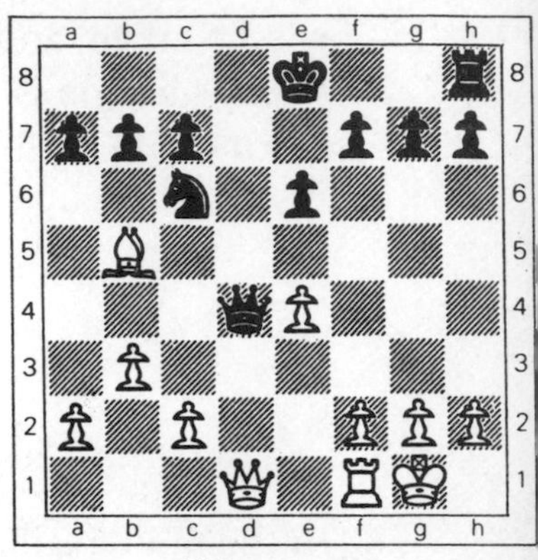
White to move

This time the black rook is needed as a defender to protect the knight. But the rook is pinned.
White will play:
Ba4xd7
But if Black retakes, his queen will be captured by White's queen.

The pin is tying down the black rook and destroying him as a useful defender.

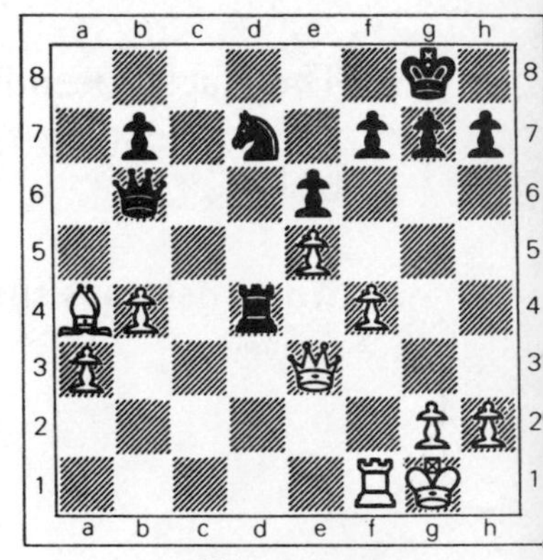
White to move

Now here are four positions for you to look at. Each time a piece can be won by a defender being destroyed.
(You can find the solutions on page 136.)

1. A white defender can be destroyed and a piece won.

What move should Black play?

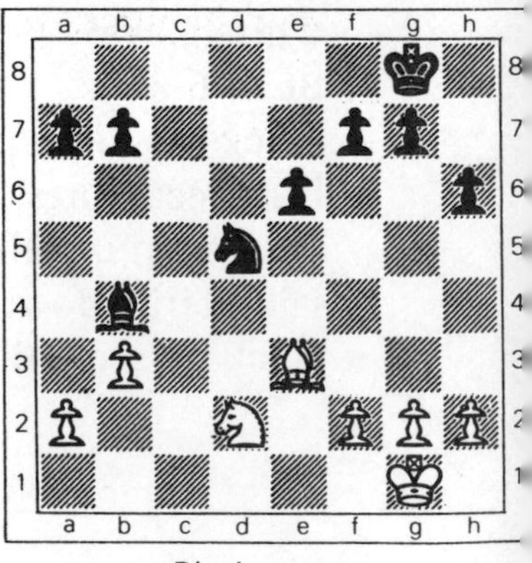
Black to move

2. One of the black men is pinned and cannot do its job as a defender properly.

What move should White play to win a piece?

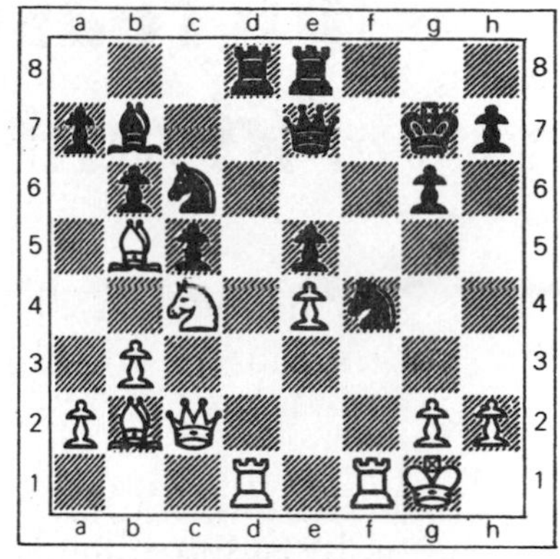

White to move

3. One of White's pieces is overloaded with work.

What move should Black play to win a piece?

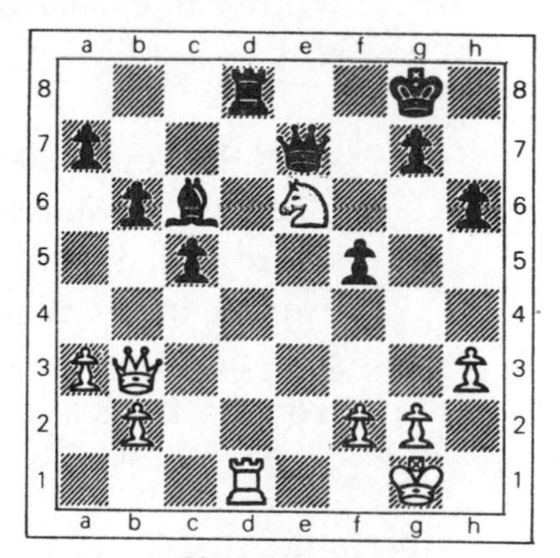

Black to move

4. The white rook is guarding its queen.

How can Black destroy the rook as a defender?

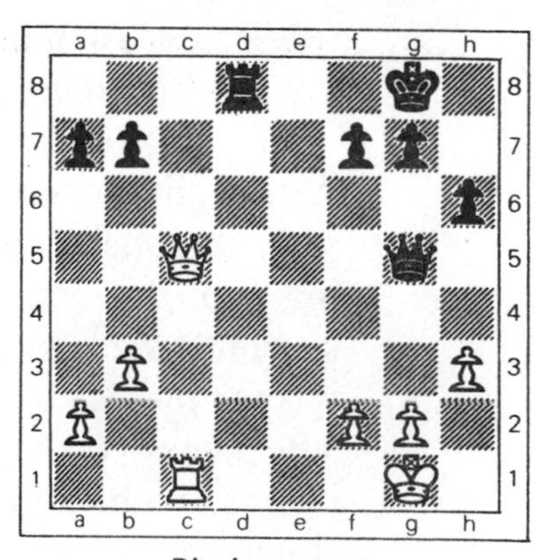

Black to move

STEP 19

Increasing Your Advantage

When you have a more powerful army than your opponent, exchange pieces whenever you can.

In this position White has the more powerful army; he is a knight ahead.

White can exchange rooks and he should do so.

With the rooks taken from the board, the black army will lose almost all of its strength. White will still have his knight, which he will use to capture Black's pawns on the Queen's side, and then he will advance his own pawn from a5 to a8 and get a queen.

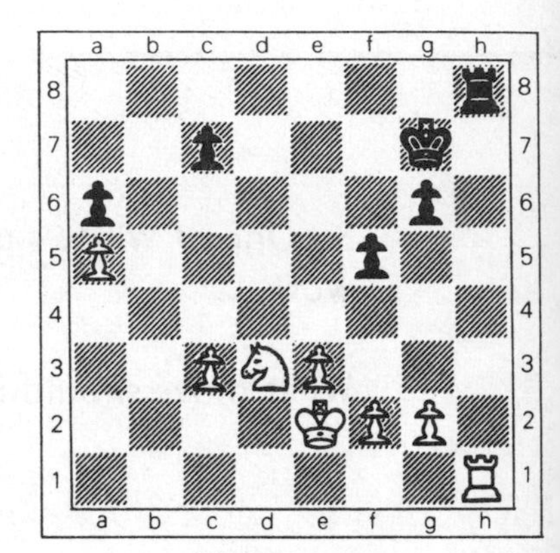

White to move

If one army has a thousand soldiers, and the other army has a thousand and five soldiers, then the armies are about equal. The extra five men will make very little difference. But a battle between one soldier on one side, and six soldiers on another, would be far from equal. The extra five men would make a lot of difference, and the one soldier would soon be finished off.

A chess battle is just the same. Whenever you exchange a piece you weaken your opponent's army. If you are winning on pieces, try to exchange as many of the remaining pieces as possible. The weaker your opponent's army becomes the less chance there will be of his fighting back. When you exchange pieces you weaken your own army, but that doesn't matter so much. The pieces you have left will be easily capable of mopping up the enemy pawns and helping you to get a queen. (The white knight will do just that in the position above, if the rooks are exchanged.).

A pawn which can march to the far end of the board without being blocked or captured by an enemy pawn is called a 'passed pawn'. A passed pawn can be a deadly weapon.

The white pawn on a4 is 'passed' because no black pawn can stop it marching on to a8.

The white pawn on h2 is not passed because it will be blocked by the black pawn on h6.

The white pawn on g2 is not passed because it can be captured by the black pawn as soon as it reaches g5.

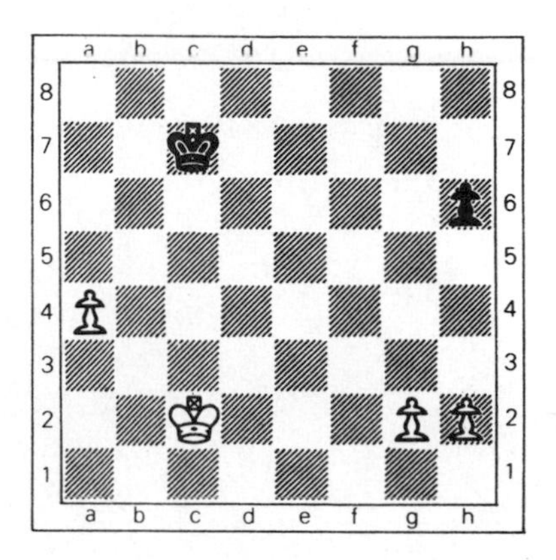

As more and more pieces get exchanged you should be on the look-out for a way to get a passed pawn, and then promote it to a queen.

In the position below White has two passed pawns, on g2 and h3, and he is a rook and three pawns ahead.

White is winning by a rook and three pawns; he should seize his chance to exchange queens.

Once the black queen has been exchanged there is little chance of Black fighting his way back into the game; without the queen his army is very weak.

White's army will also be queenless, but he has two passed pawns which he can advance, and he will soon be threatening to regain his queen.

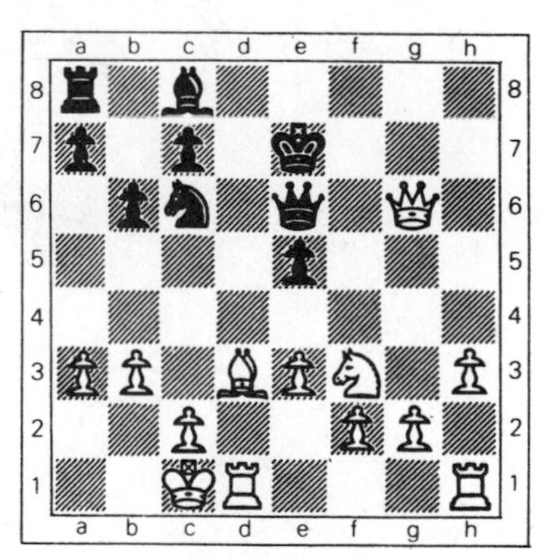

White to move

Increase your advantage! Exchange pieces, win the enemy pawns, get a passed pawn, get a new queen, get checkmate! It's simple!

STEP 20

Checkmating the Lone King

Winning pieces is a great help, but to win the game you still have to get checkmate. This is what we will do now: look at ways of checkmating when we have an advantage in pieces. To begin with we will make things simpler by imagining that we have captured all of our opponent's men, and he has only his king left on the board.

Before you begin your checkmating attack you must have a plan. There is no point in aimlessly checking your opponent's king all round the board in the hope that luck will be with you and one of the aimless checks will just happen to be checkmate. No matter what pieces you have on the board for your checkmating attack, there is one general plan which you should always follow:

The enemy king must be pushed back to the edge of the board and then surrounded by the attacking pieces.

If you attack the king, he will run away. If you attack him again, he will run away again. However, when he gets to the edge of the board he's like a boxer driven back on the ropes; he can't run any further, he has to stand and fight. But unlike the boxer the poor king has little to fight with, he is more or less defenceless, and checkmating him is easy.

The queen and rook are the most useful pieces for checkmating, so we will concentrate on them. Remember that after the last pawn move or capture has been made you have fifty moves in which to get checkmate. If you don't get checkmate in those fifty moves the game is drawn. Don't let this worry you. Fifty moves is an enormous number, and if you follow the plan for checkmate, you will always catch the king quickly and easily.

Checkmate with two Rooks
The usual sort of checkmating position⟶

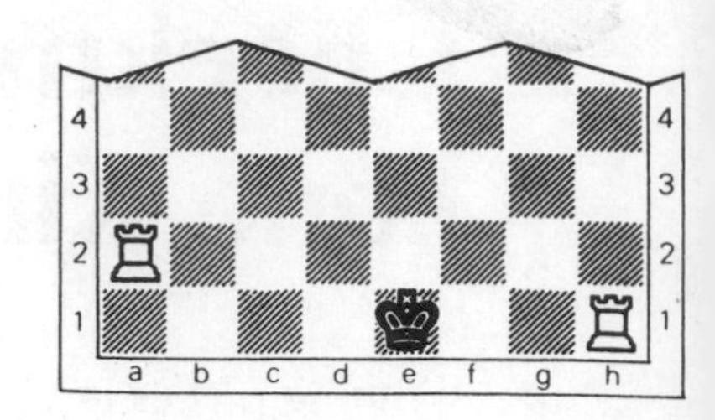

The black king is trapped at the edge of the board.

The white rooks attack along the two ranks the king might try to use for escape.

How to do it!

First we must decide to which edge of the board we are going to drive the black king. It doesn't matter which edge we choose.

In this position the king is nearest the top edge of the board; so it would be quickest to drive him up the page.

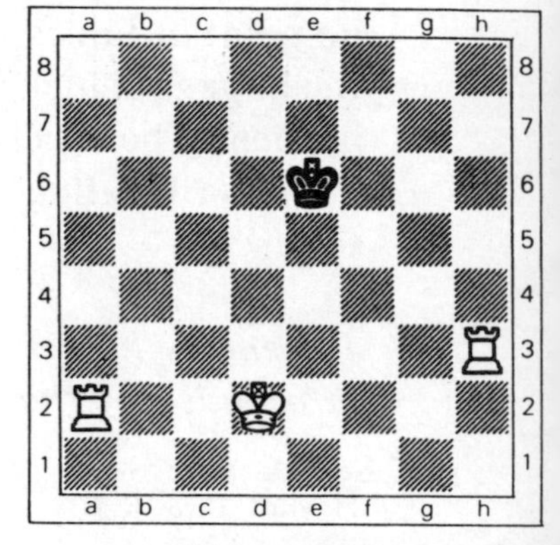

White to move

Second we must stop the king from going the other way. We don't want the king to escape down the board; so we must put a rook (it doesn't matter which) on rank 5.
We will play:
1 Ra2-a5

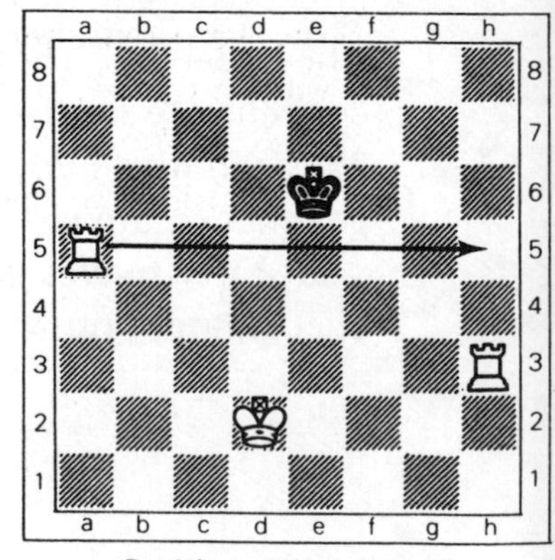

Position after 1 Ra2-a5

The black king is now trapped on the back three ranks. He cannot come forward because the white rook attacks all the squares on rank 5. He must go sideways or backwards.

We will suppose Black plays:

1 ... Ke6-d6

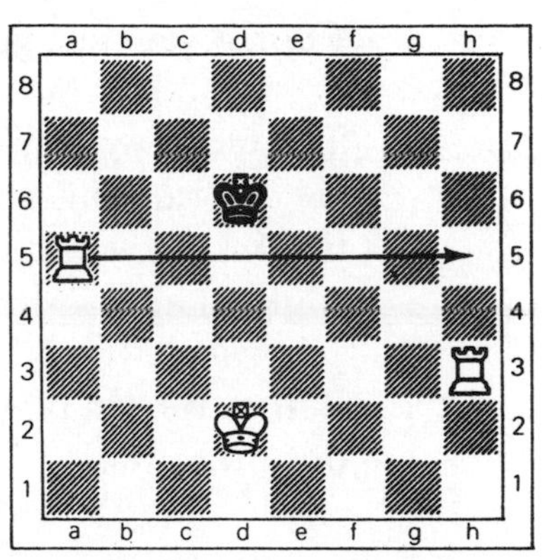

Position after 1 . . . Ke6-d6

Third we must drive the king to the edge of the board by checking him.

The rook on a5 is doing a useful job, stopping the king escaping down the board. The rook on h3 is doing nothing; so we will use it for checking:

2 Rh3-h6+

The black king cannot remain on rank 6; he cannot come forward to rank 5; he must go back:

2 ... Kd6-c7

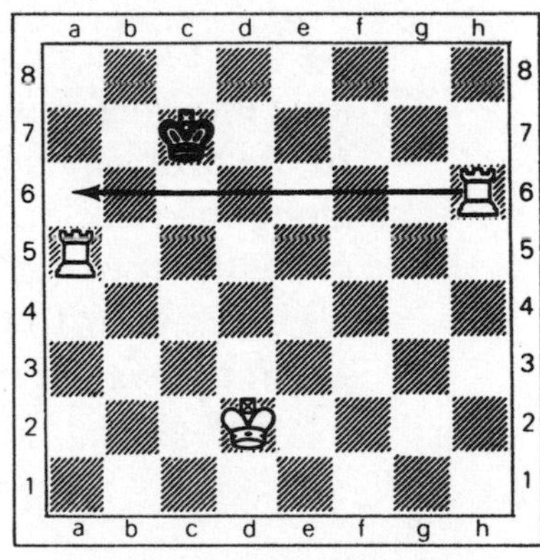

Position after 2 . . . Kd6-c7

Now we must check again. We must keep a rook on rank 6 to stop the king escaping down the board, but the rook on a5 is no longer doing anything; so we will use it for checking:

3 Ra5-a7+

Now the king must retreat to the edge of the board.

3 ... Kc7-b8

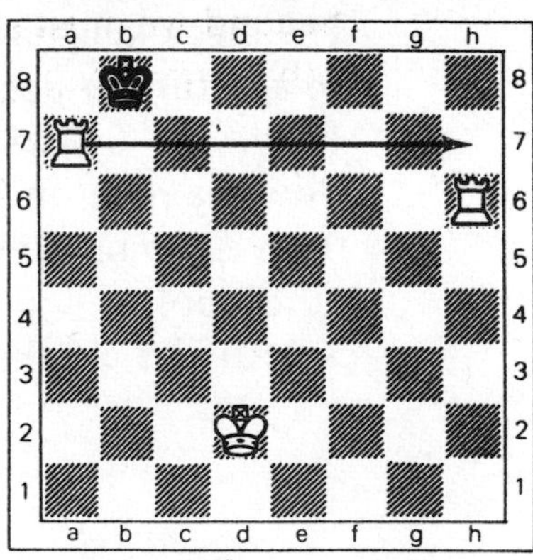

Position after 3 . . . Kc7-b8

Fourth we must get checkmate.

The move we want to play is Rh6-h8+, but we can't do this straight away because the black king would escape by capturing the rook on a7.

Before we can play Rh6-h8 we must save our other rook.

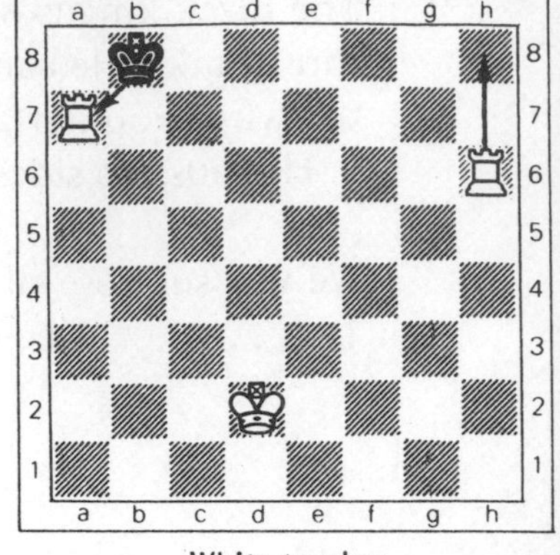

White to play

We must keep a rook on rank 7 to stop the king escaping down the board. The answer to the problem is to move the rook from a7, along the rank, to a safe square. We want to move the rook right away from the king, but we don't want to put it on h7 where it would get in the way of our other rook:

4 Ra7-g7

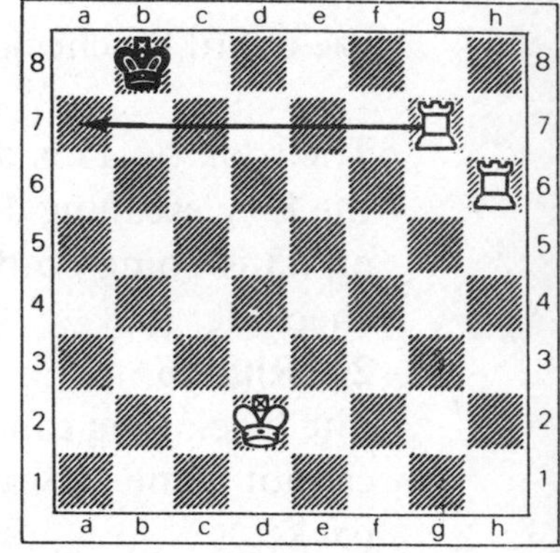

Position after 4 Ra7-g7

The black king has run out of board! He can't go any further backwards.

4 . . . Kb8-c8

Now the rook on g7 is stopping the king from escaping; so we give checkmate with the other rook:

5 Rh6-h8 checkmate

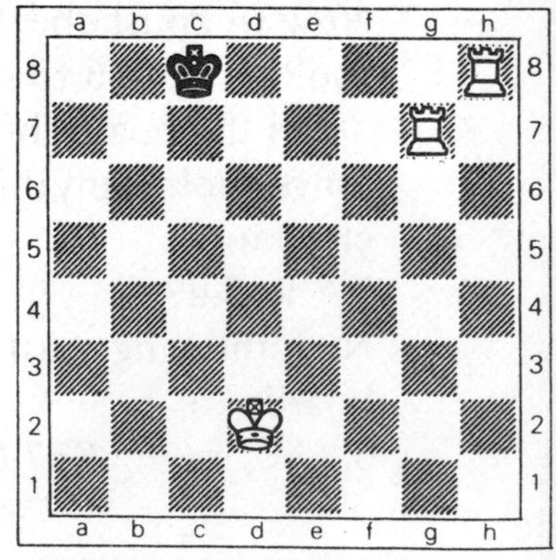

Position after 5 Rh6-h8 checkmate

Checkmate with one Rook

The usual sort of checkmating position ⟶

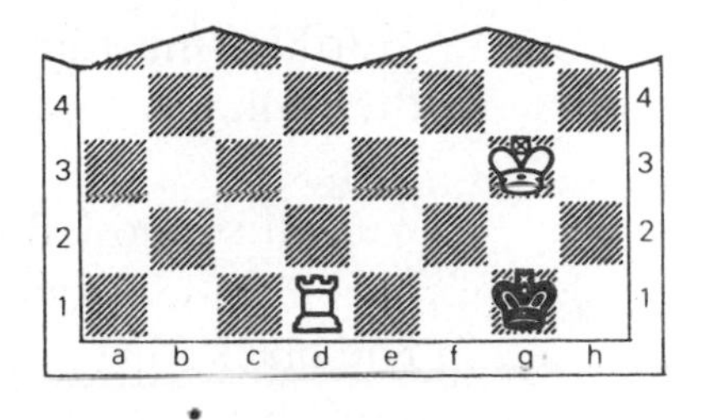

The black king is trapped at the edge of the board.

The white king stops him from moving forward and escaping.

How to do it!

First we must decide to which corner of the board we are going to drive the black king. It doesn't matter which corner we choose.

In this position the king is nearest the top right-hand corner of the board, so it would be quickest to drive him there.

White to move

Second we must stop the king from going the other way. We must shut the king inside a small rectangle of squares from which he cannot escape.

We will play:

1 Re2-e5

The black king is now trapped in the top right-hand corner; he cannot escape over either of the lines attacked by the rook.

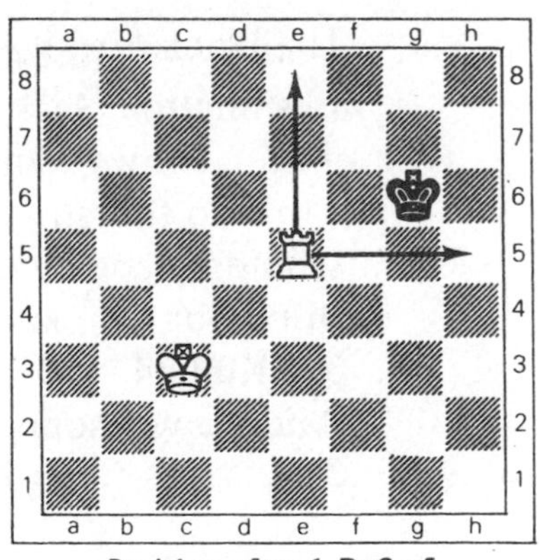

Position after 1 Re2-e5

Third we must bring up our own king to help the rook.

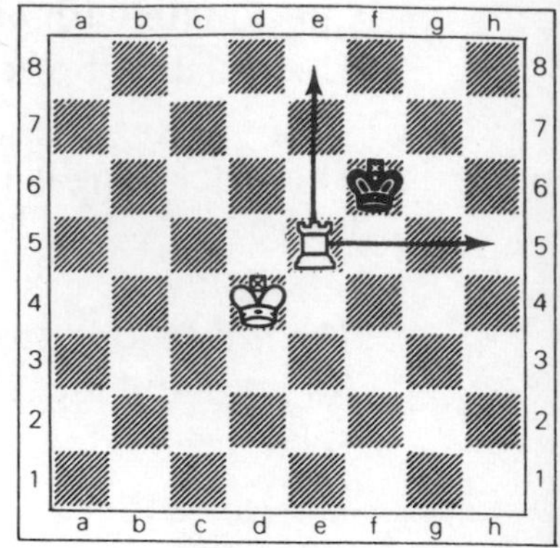
Position after 2 Kc3-d4

We will suppose Black plays:

1 . . . Kg6-f6

The black king is attacking our rook. We don't want to move the rook because it is doing a useful job shutting the black king inside the rectangle.

Our king must come and help:

2 Kc3-d4

There are nine squares the black king can use, he cannot escape from the rectangle.

We will suppose Black plays:

2 . . . Kf6-g6

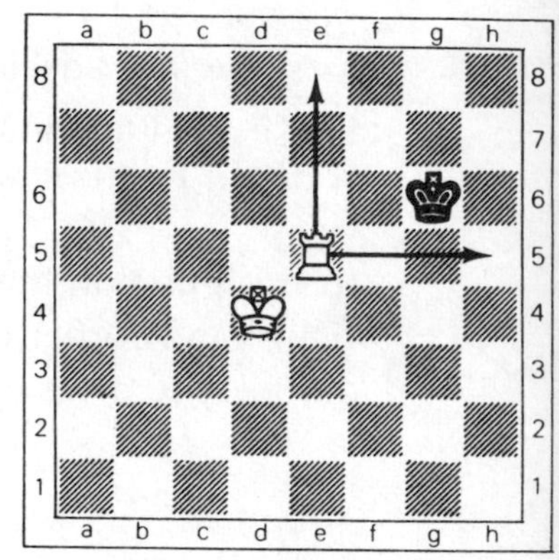
Position after 2 . . . Kf6-g6

Fourth we must make the rectangle smaller, pushing the black king into the corner.

The move we want to play is Re5-f5 but we can't do this straight away because the king would escape by capturing the rook. We must bring our own king closer:

3 Kd4-e4

And we will suppose Black plays:

3 . . . Kg6-f6

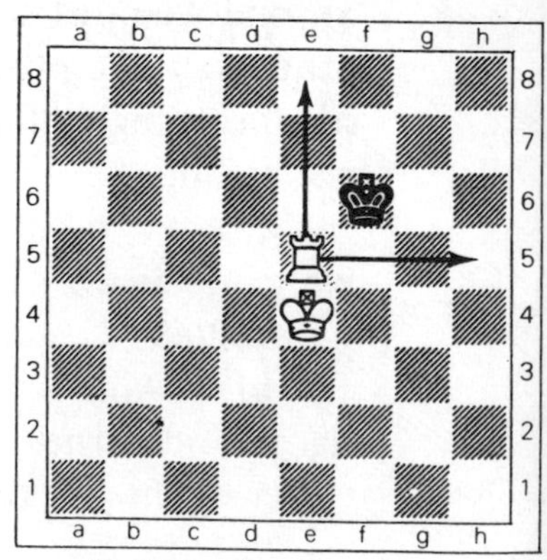
Position after 3 . . . Kg6-f6

We still don't want to move the rook to f5 because the black king could go to e6 and escape from the rectangle. So we *don't* check. Instead we must spend another move with our king:

4 Ke4-f4

We will suppose Black plays:

4 . . . Kf6-g6

And now we can make the rectangle smaller:

5 Re5-f5

The black king is now trapped inside a rectangle of only six squares.

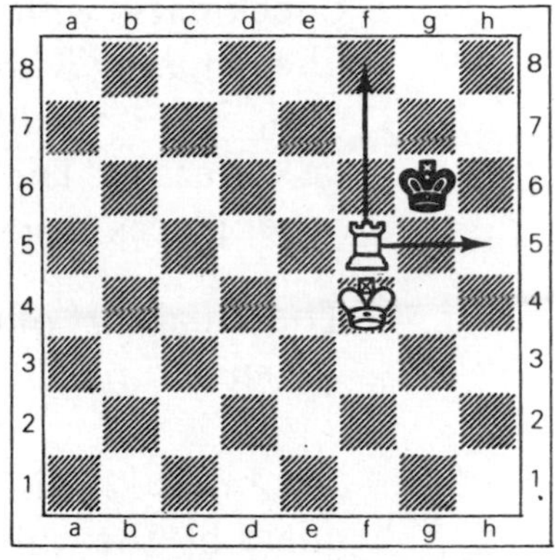

Position after 5 Re5-f5

Suppose Black plays:

5 . . . Kg6-g7

We bring our king closer:

6 Kf4-g5

Black plays:

6 . . . Kg7-h7

We make the rectangle smaller:

7 Rf5-f7+

Black must retreat:

7 . . . Kh7-g8

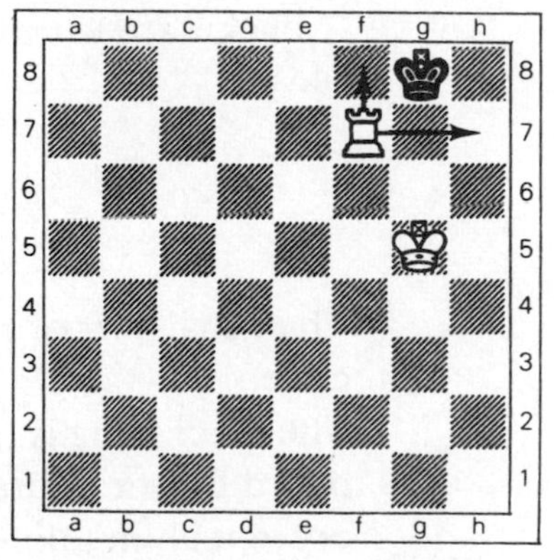

Position after 7 . . . Kh7-g8

The black king is trapped at the edge of the board in a rectangle of only two squares.

We bring our king closer:

8 Kg5-g6

Black has no choice:

8 . . . Kg8-h8

And our rook gives checkmate:

9 Rf7-f8 checkmate

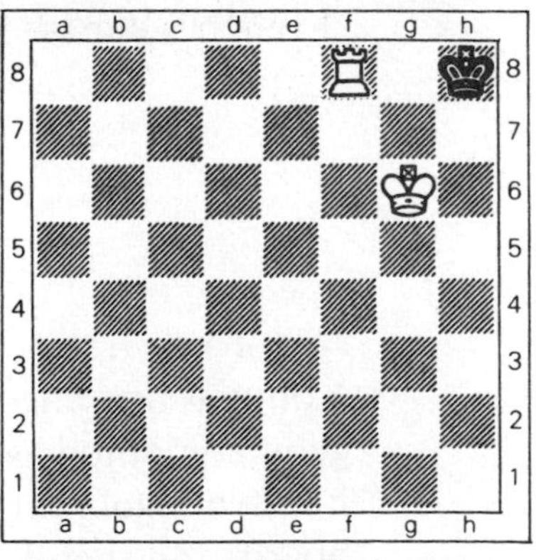

Position after 9 Rf7-f8 checkmate

Checkmates with the Queen

Checkmating with the queen is really just the same as checkmating with a rook. The only difference is that because the queen is more powerful, the task is easier. The queen attacks more squares, the enemy king will have fewer places to go, and there will be more checkmating positions.

The usual sort of checkmating positions with queen and rook:

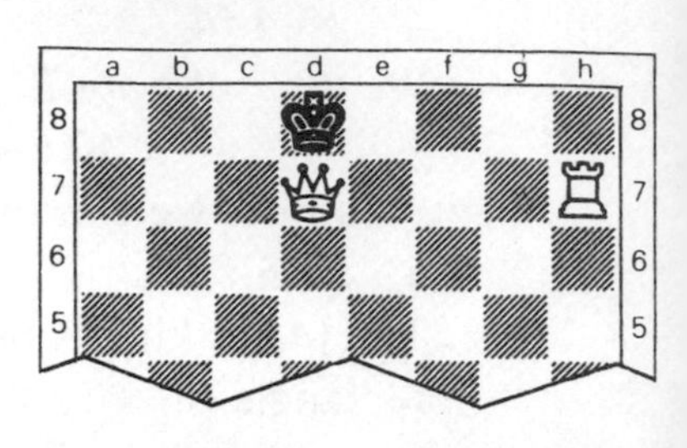

The black king is nailed to the edge of the board by the white queen. The rook prevents him taking the queen and escaping.

The same checkmating position as for 'Checkmate with two Rooks'.

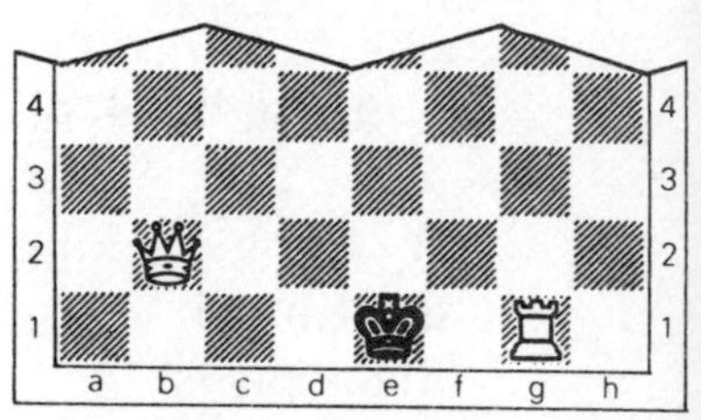

The usual sort of checkmating positions with queen:
The black king is nailed to the edge of the board by the white queen. The white king prevents him taking the queen and escaping.

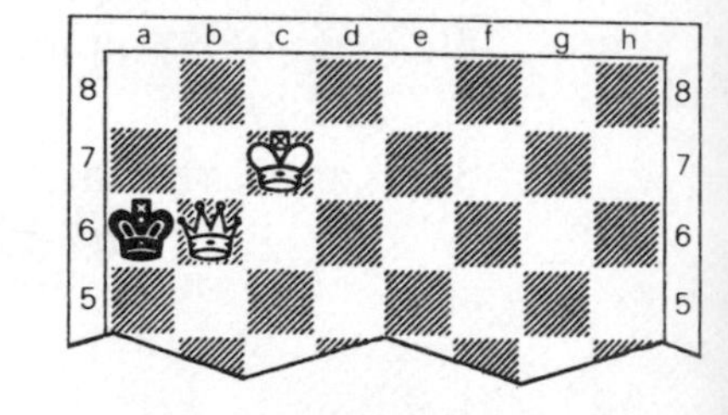

The same checkmating position as for 'Checkmate with one Rook'.

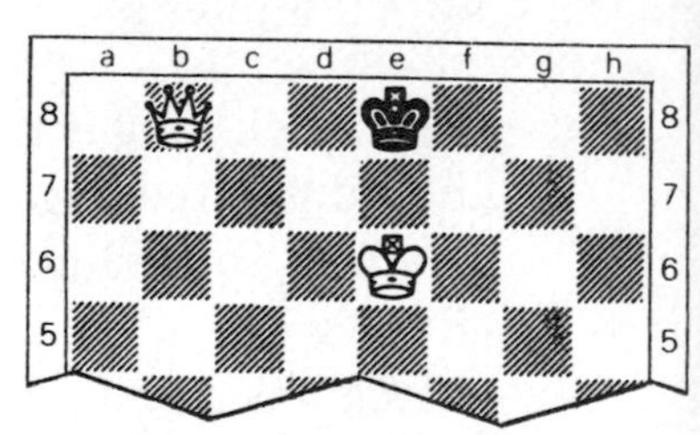

How to do it!

You will find checkmates with the queen easy so long as you follow the general method as before. Decide where you want to drive the king, stop him from going anywhere else, gradually push him back to the edge of the board, and then finish him off!

Checkmate with the Minor Pieces
The plan for checkmating with bishops and knights is to drive the king into a corner. This isn't easy to do, but don't worry. You will play thousands of games without ever having to checkmate with just the minor pieces.

Sensible Ideas for Checkmate

We have been checkmating the lone king, but you won't wait until you have captured all of your opponent's men. You will be looking for checkmate much earlier in the game.

Set up this position on your board, and look at it for a few moments.

White is winning easily; he is a queen and knight ahead.

To win, White has got to get checkmate. How should White set about mating his opponent's king?

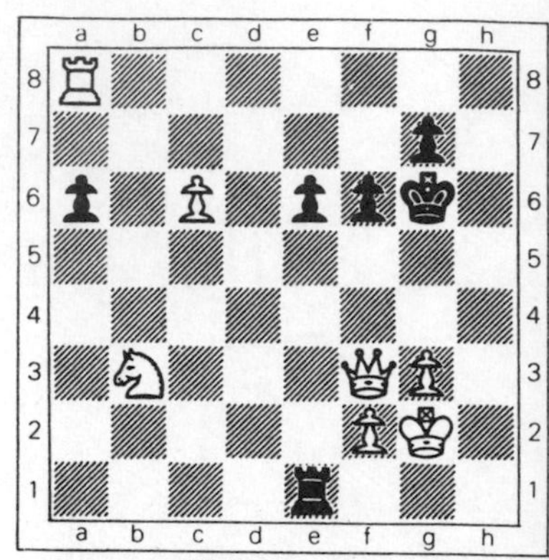

White to move

White could play Ra8xa6. But does White need to win another black pawn?

Of course not.

White wants to get checkmate.

The black pawn is useless; unless it advances and threatens to become a queen, White can ignore it; capturing would be a waste of time.

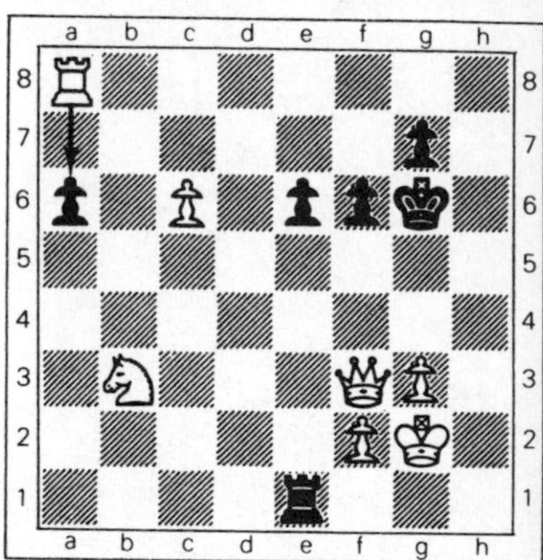

White to move

White could steadily advance his pawn from c6 to c8 and get another queen. But does White need another queen?

Of course not.

White already has enough pieces to get checkmate; advancing his pawn to get another queen would be a waste of time.

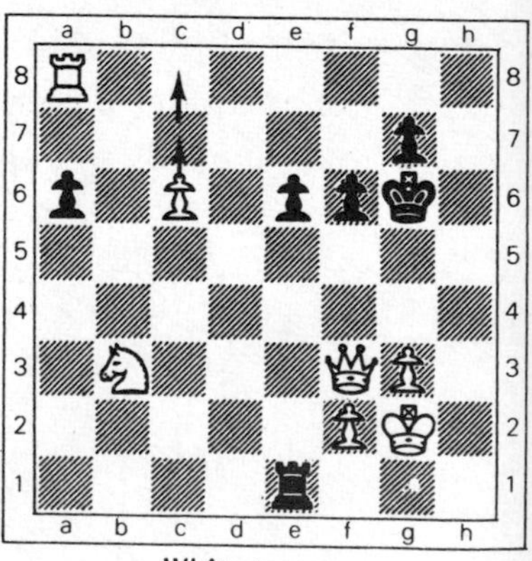

White to move

White could bring his knight over towards the black king. But does White need his knight for the checkmating attack?

Of course not.

The white queen and rook are quite capable of rounding up the black king; the white knight might even get in the way!

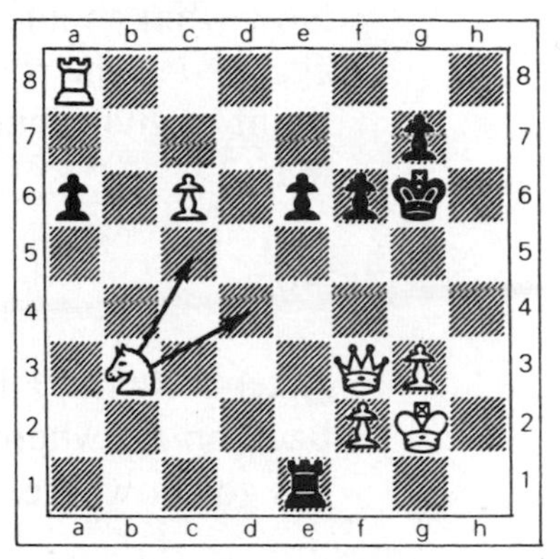

White to move

White must find a plan. He must use the strength of his queen and rook to surround the black king, and he must get straight on with the job.

White should play:

1 Qf3-g4+

. . . hitting the enemy straight away. The black king must run . . .

1 . . . Kg6-f7

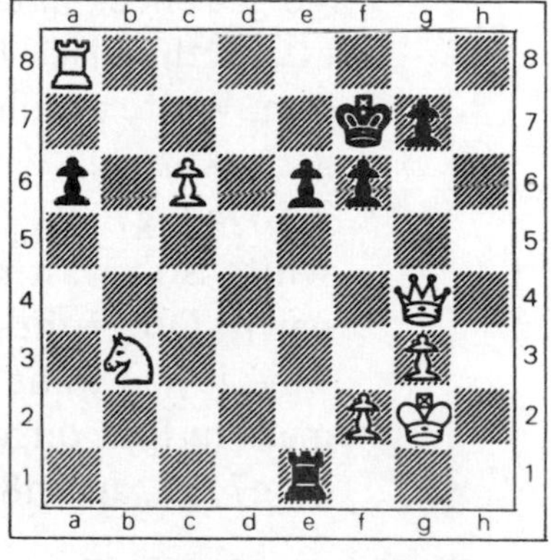

Position after 1 . . . Kg6-f7

The white queen won't be able to force checkmate on her own, so the rook must come into the attack . . .

2 Ra8-a7+

. . . and the black king must keep running . . .

2 . . . Kf7-e8

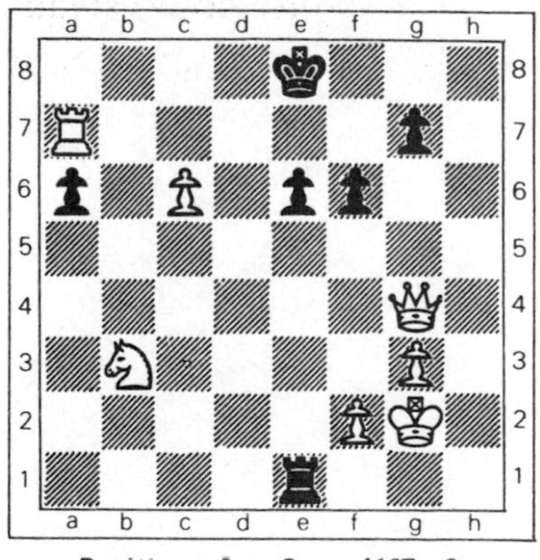

Position after 2 . . . Kf7-e8

White to move

Now what should White do? He could check again with the rook on a8. But is there any point in giving check? Does it help get checkmate?

No.

After 3 Ra7-a8+ Black simply puts his king back on f7, where it came from, and White has got nowhere.

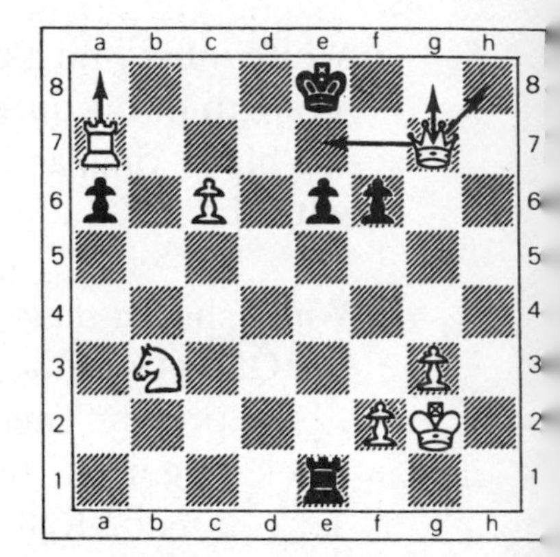
Position after 3 Qg4xg7

To get checkmate White has not just got to attack the black king; he has got to surround him. White should bring his queen back into action . . .

3 Qg4xg7

White isn't wasting time capturing this black pawn! On g7 the pawn stood smack in White's way; it had to be taken. Now White threatens mate in four different places, with his queen on e7, g8, and h8, and with his rook on a8.

The black king can't escape.

Let us sum up the ideas:

1. *Checkmate wins a game of chess.*
You should be on the look-out for a chance to checkmate your opponent at every move, right from the beginning of the game. When you have a big advantage in pieces your mind should be fixed firmly on checkmating your opponent as quickly as possible. Find a plan. Decide which pieces are best placed and most powerful for the mating attack, and get on with the job.

2. *Don't waste time winning useless pawns; capture only those that stand between you and checkmate.*
You win a game by getting checkmate. You don't get a special prize for being clever enough to win all of your opponent's pieces. Once you have a lead in pieces it is often easy to win more. If your opponent's pawns stand between you and his king, then smash them aside by capturing. But never hold up your mating attack; never go out of your way just for the fun of wiping out the enemy army. Get on with the job of checkmating.

3. *Don't make a collection of unnecessary queens.*
Once you have a big lead in pieces it is usually easy to push pawns through and gain more queens. Why bother? If you have enough pieces to force checkmate, then you don't need more queens. Nobody will think you clever because you have three queens on the board—they might think you're a bit daft because you can't finish the enemy off with less!

4. *Don't check for the sake of checking.*
When you give check you are only attacking your opponent's king, and there may be several ways in which he can escape. To get checkmate you have to surround and trap him. You don't gain anything by checking unless it helps you get checkmate. Don't check for the sake of checking, and just drive your opponent's king aimlessly around the board.

5. *Don't let your own pieces get in your way.*
Your queen and rooks are the best pieces for the mating attack. Sometimes the king is useful, but the bishops and knights are much weaker and slower moving. When you have a big advantage in pieces let your queen and rooks do the work of mating, and don't allow your other pieces to get in their way.

ROUND
1

STEP 21

The Opening

How does a general plan a big battle? Does he just turn up with all of his men, and let them charge off as they like into the attack? Of course not!

He must plan the battle carefully. He must decide where on the battlefield his men will be most powerfully placed.

You must make the same decisions at the chess-board. Each of your pieces must be brought into play; placed on a square where it can help you attack and defend. The first few moves of the game, when the pieces are preparing for battle, is called the **Opening**.

The opening is very important; if you can quickly bring your pieces into play on good squares you will soon be ready to attack.
There are several ideas worth remembering in the opening. We will play through a game and talk about them as we go along, so get your board ready for the start.

1 e2-e4
A splendid move.

Now White can bring both his queen and his light-squared bishop into the game.

It is always a good idea to have a pawn in the middle of the board.

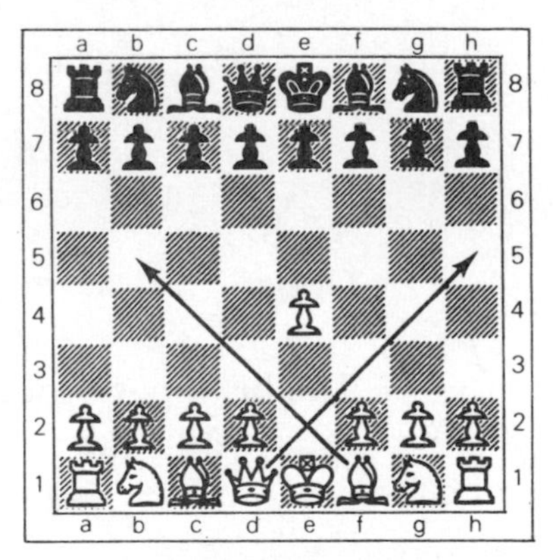

Position after 1 e2-e4

1 . . . e7-e5

Black plays this good move for the same reasons.

Position after 2 Ng1-f3

2 Ng1-f3

Another good move.

The knight is brought into battle and attacks Black's e-pawn.

2 . . . f7-f6

A bad move.

On f6 the pawn blocks in its own queen and stands in the way of its knight.

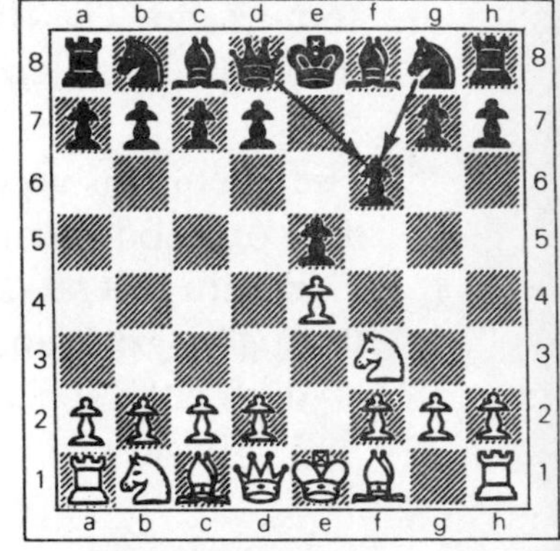

Position after 2 . . . f7-f6

3 Bf1-c4

Good!

The bishop is brought into the game on a fine square near the centre.

3 . . . Ng8-h6

Bad!

The knight is brought into the game, but it is stuck on a poor square right on the edge of the board.

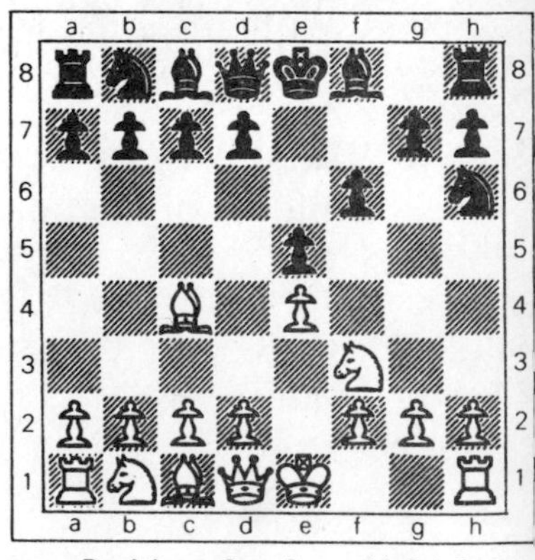

Position after 3 . . . Ng8-h6

4 d2-d3

White is getting ready to bring his other bishop into battle.

Black takes his chance to attack the white king:

4 . . . Bf8-b4+

But this is a poor move.

The bishop is brought into play, but he will soon be driven back.

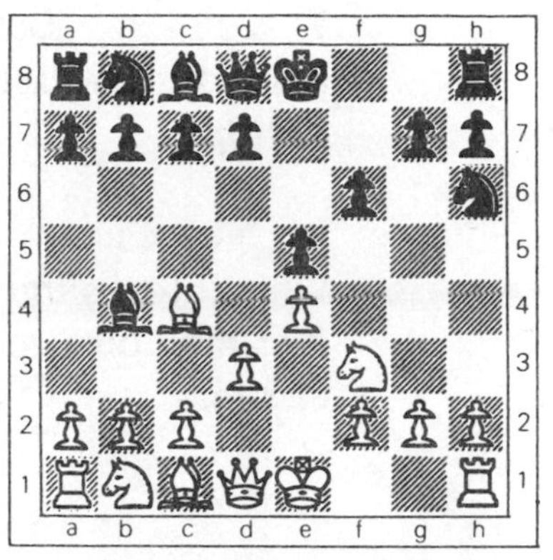

Position after 4 . . . Bf8-b4+

5 c2-c3

White easily escapes from check, and attacks the black bishop.

The bishop must run away:

5 . . . Bb4-c5

Black has wasted time.

Black has taken two moves to get his bishop from f8 to c5.

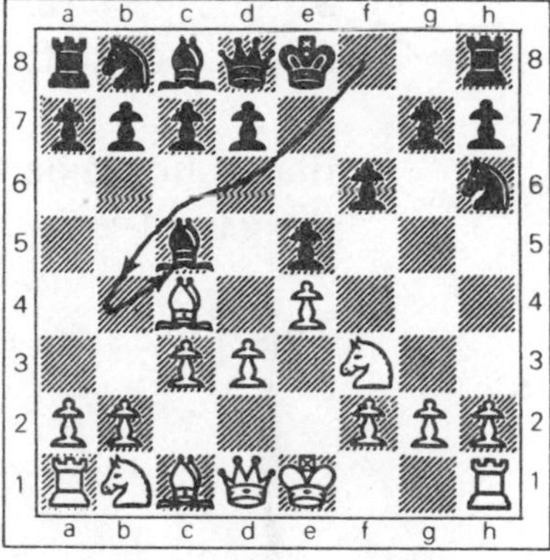

Position after 5 . . . Bb4-c5

White now has the chance to put another pawn in the centre, and win space for his pieces:

6 d3-d4 e5xd4

7 c3xd4

White has made room to bring his queen, his dark-squared bishop, and his other knight into the game.

And . . . the black bishop is attacked again!

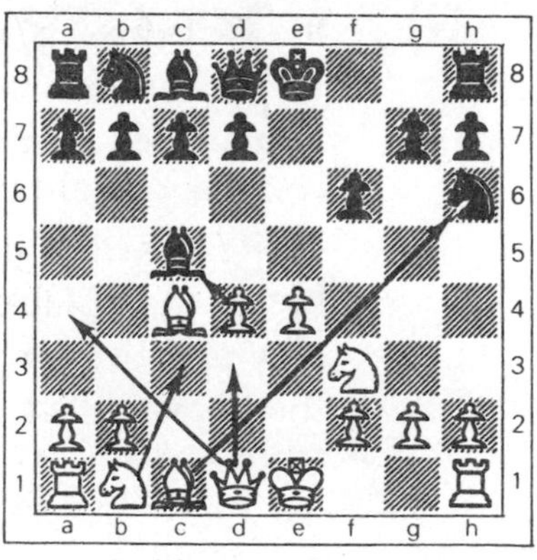

Position after 7 c3xd4

7 . . . Bc5-b4+
Black has to waste another move to save his bishop.

8 Nb1-c3
White blocks the check, and brings his knight into play on a good square aiming at the centre.

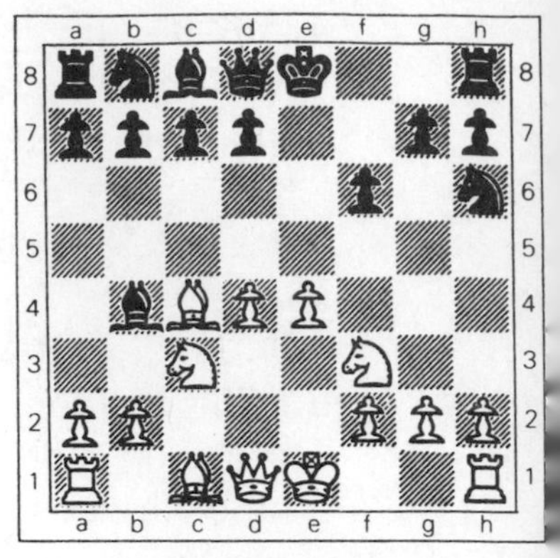
Position after 8 Nb1-c3

8 . . . a7-a6
A really dreadful move!

Black should be trying to bring his pieces into the game.

This move does nothing to help him.

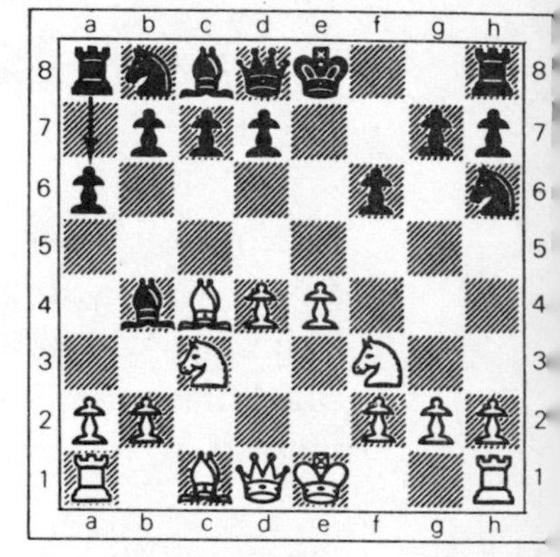
Position after 8 . . . a7-a6

9 Bc1xh6 g7xh6
White has exchanged a bishop, which was not in play, for a knight, which was.

White has been playing the opening much better than Black. White has three pieces in play and two strong pawns in the middle of the board. Black has only one piece in play.

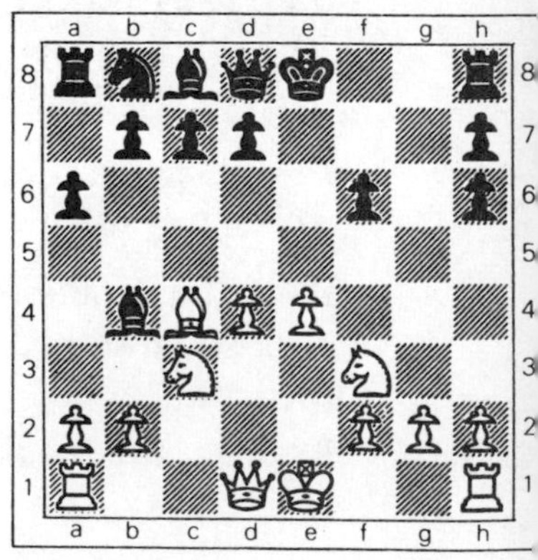
Position after 9 . . . g7xh6

The white pieces are ready to attack, the black pieces are not ready to defend.

10 Nf3-h4

The knight makes way for the white queen to come to h5.

The knight is not very well placed on h4, right on the edge of the board, but he will be able to come back into action on f5.

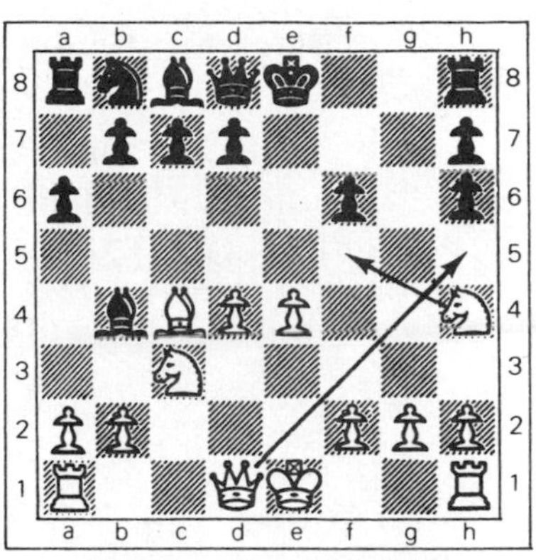

Position after 10 Nf3-h4

10 ... Nb8-c6

At last Black brings one of his pieces into play on a good square . . . but it is already far too late.

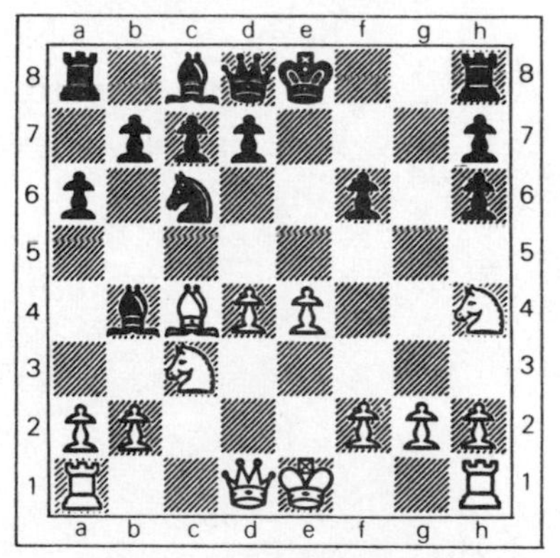

Position after 10 . . . Nb8-c6

11 Qd1-h5+

The white queen swings into action and attacks the black king.

White's knight and bishop are ready, waiting to add their power to the attack.

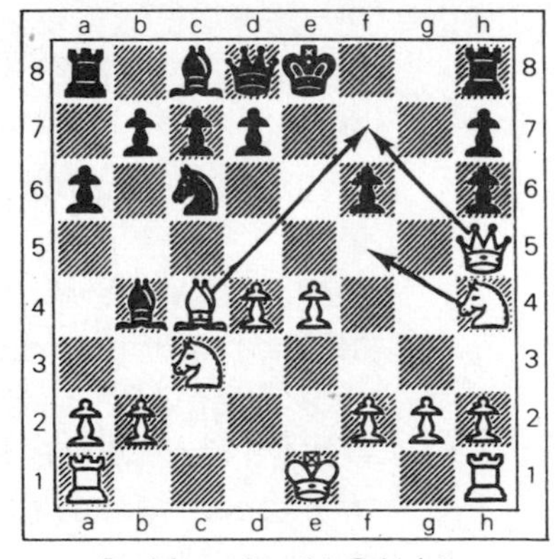

Position after 11 Qd1-h5+

Black must move his king:

11 . . . Ke8-e7

White has too many pieces in play; he will quickly surround the black king.

12 Qh5-f7+

Position after 12 Qh5-f7+

12 . . . Ke7-d6

13 Nh4-f5 mate

White's pieces have neatly tied up the black king!

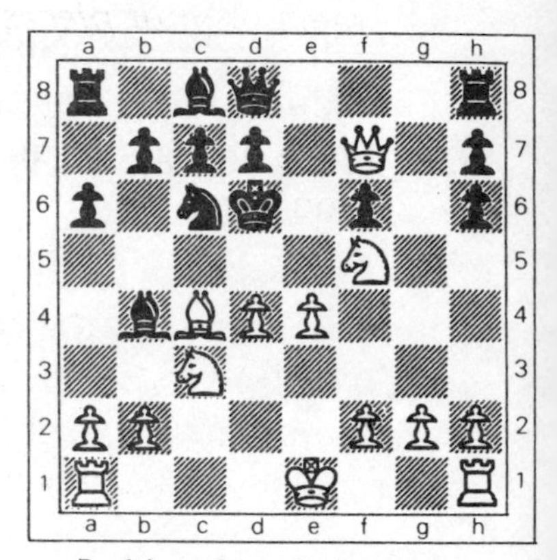

Position after 13 Nh4-f5 mate

White has won!

Why?

Because White played the opening better.

Why?

Because White quickly brought his pieces into play on good squares, while Black really just messed around doing nothing.

The opening is a race.

The player who is first to bring his pieces into play on good squares, wins the race. He will have the first chance to attack, he will be ready to defend.

What is a 'good square'?

A good square is one from which the piece will be able to leap into the attack or come to the defence. The piece should be in, or aimed at, the centre of the board, because a piece in the centre is generally far more powerful than one stuck at the side of the board.

Black lost!
Why?
Because he didn't bring his pieces into play quickly enough, and he didn't put them on good squares.

You must remember and follow the one golden rule of the opening:
Each of your pieces must be brought quickly into play on a good square.

Now we have looked at the general ideas behind the opening we will list a few rules worth following.

Pawns
Put a pawn in the centre and keep it there if you can; if you can do this you will find that your pieces will get more room to move around. Only make pawn moves which will help you to bring your pieces into play. Don't put pawns on squares where they will get in the way of your pieces.

Pieces
Find a good square for each piece.
Make sure the piece is safe, and cannot easily be driven away.
Remember the opening is a race. Don't waste time wandering around the board with one piece while you still have others waiting to be brought into play.
Aim your pieces at the centre of the board; in the centre they should be able to move easily and powerfully in any direction.
Don't put pieces on the edge of the board unless you have no choice.
Don't start to attack until your pieces are ready to join in the battle.

Remember
Each of your pieces must be brought quickly into play on a good square.

There are many common ways of starting a game; openings with strange and fancy names. There are many books on the opening, full of moves you could learn. To begin with the important thing is not to learn a lot of opening moves, but to remember the ideas we have listed on the last page.

There are, however, one or two things you should know:

The quickest way you can lose a game is two moves:

1	**f2-f3**	**e7-e5**
2	**g2-g4**	**Qd8-h4 mate**

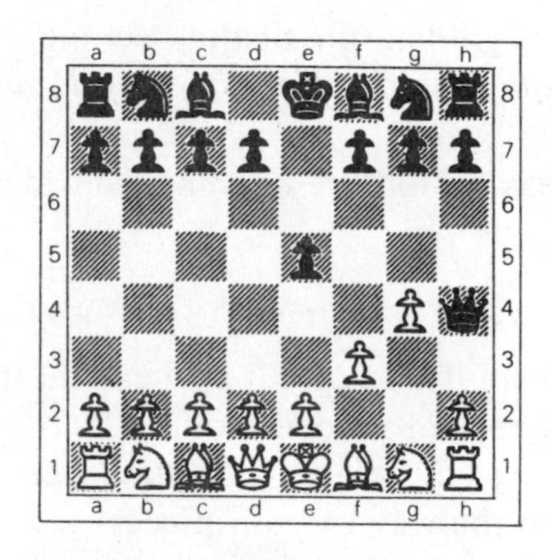

This is called ‘Fool’s Mate’.

White has paid for his two silly pawn moves.

Let’s hope you are never a ‘Fool’.

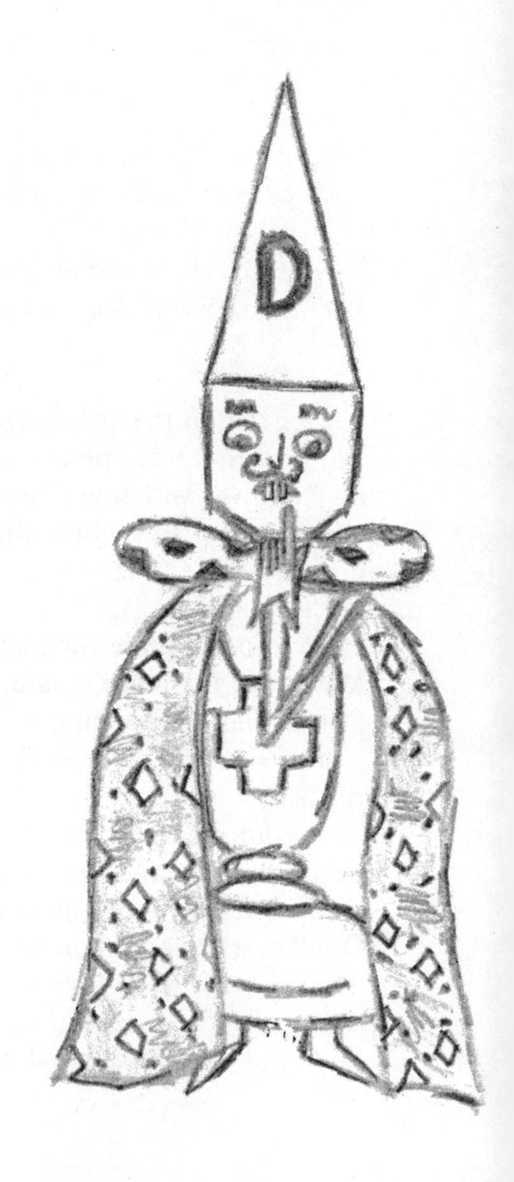

Another quick checkmate is the four-move 'Scholar's Mate'.
You may be threatened with Scholar's Mate quite often; so you must know how to deal with it.

The weak point in your position at the start of the game is your f-pawn; it stands right next to your king, and it is defended only by your king.

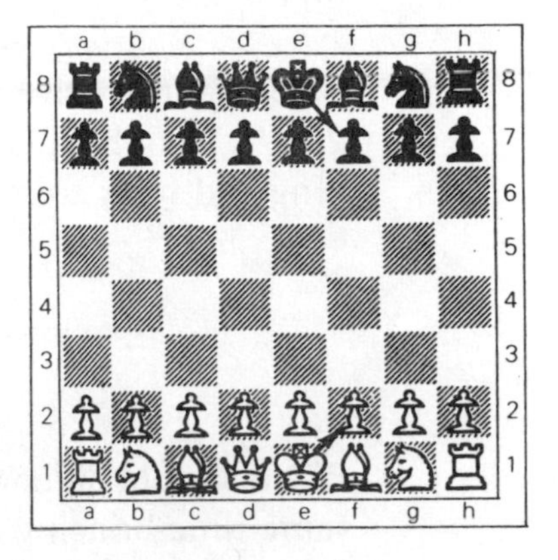

The idea behind Scholar's Mate is to attack the f-pawn with a queen and a bishop:

1 e2-e4
2 Bf1-c4
3 Qd1-h5 or Qd1-f3
4 Qh5xf7 or Qf3xf7
Checkmate!

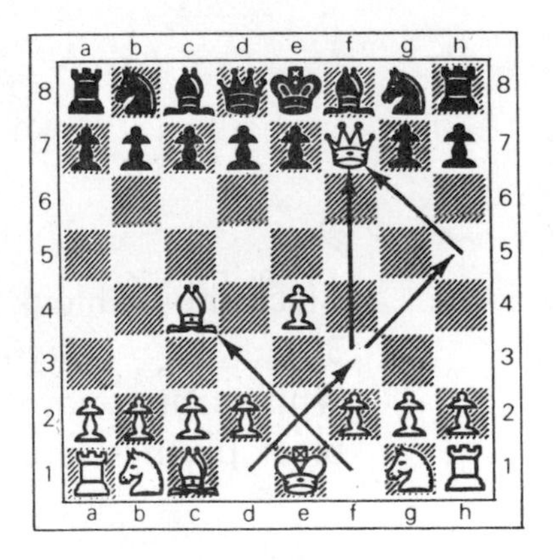

It looks very simple, doesn't it?
Both players should be careful that they don't get caught like this at the start of the game. But there is nothing to worry about. As we shall see, Scholar's Mate is easy to answer.

Play these moves on your board:
1 **e2-e4** **e7-e5**
2 **Qd1-h5**
White is getting ready to threaten Scholar's Mate.

Black cannot drive the white queen away by 2 . . . g7-g6; because of 3 Qh5xe5+ and his king and rook are forked.

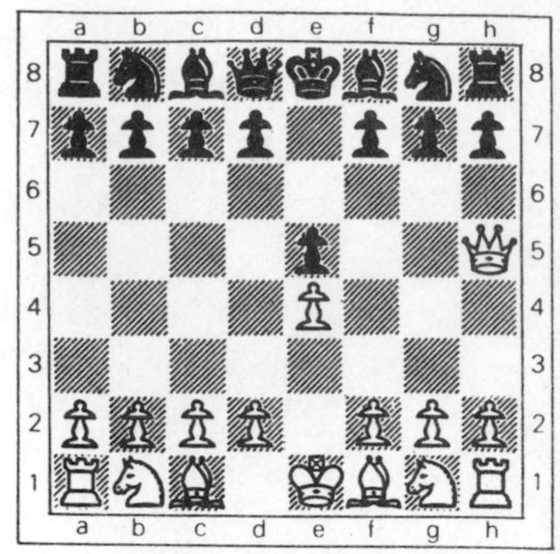
Position after 2 Qd1-h5

Black should defend his e-pawn while at the same time bringing a piece into play:
2 **. . .** **Nb8-c6**
3 **Bf1-c4**
And now White threatens 4 Qh5xf7 mate.

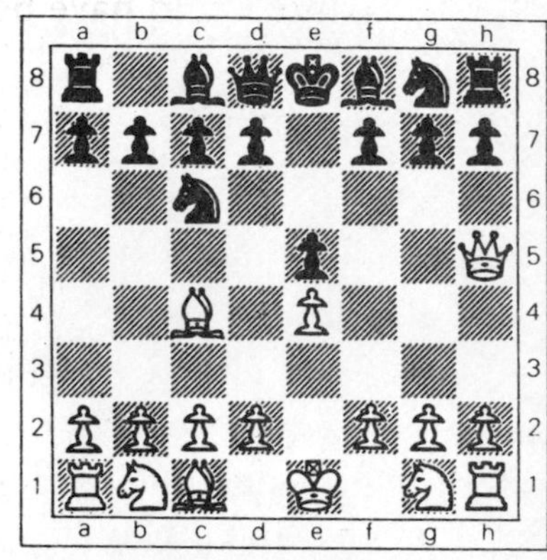
Position after 3 Bf1-c4

Black should block this threat with:
3 **. . .** **g7-g6**
White cannot now capture on e5 because the black pawn is defended by the knight on c6.

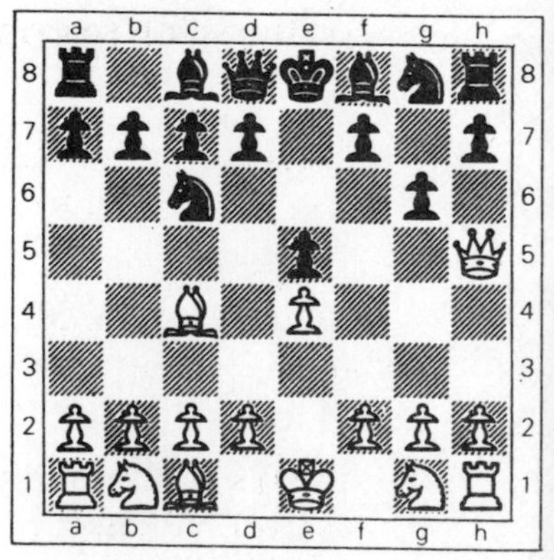
Position after 3 . . . g7-g6

White's only way to threaten mate again is by:

4 Qh5-f3

But now Black can simply bring out another piece:

4 . . . Ng8-f6

. . . and block the queen's attack again.

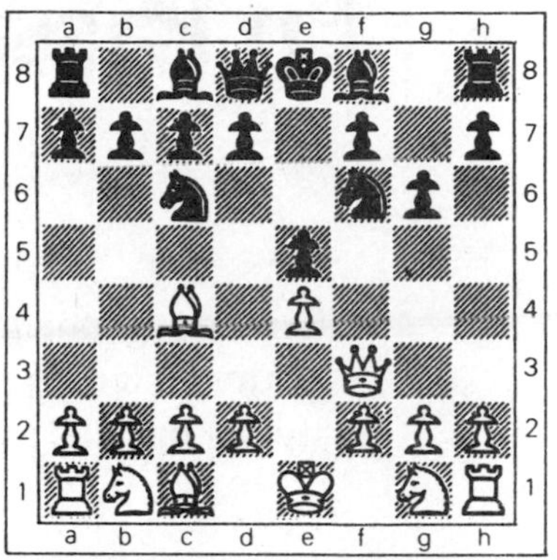

Position after 4 . . . Ng8-f6

White could have begun his Scholar's Mate attack by playing Qd1-f3 or Bf1-c4 on move 2, instead of Qd1-h5. Don't worry! Simply play 2 . . . Nb8-c6 and then block the mate threat by 3 . . . g7-g6 or 3 . . . Ng8-f6, whichever is necessary.

The move . . . Ng8-f6 is always useful for Black in the opening.

It stops the white queen going to g4 or h5.
It blocks an attack along the file to f7.
It attacks e4 and d5, two good squares in the centre.

Of course, a white knight on f3 is well placed for the same reasons.

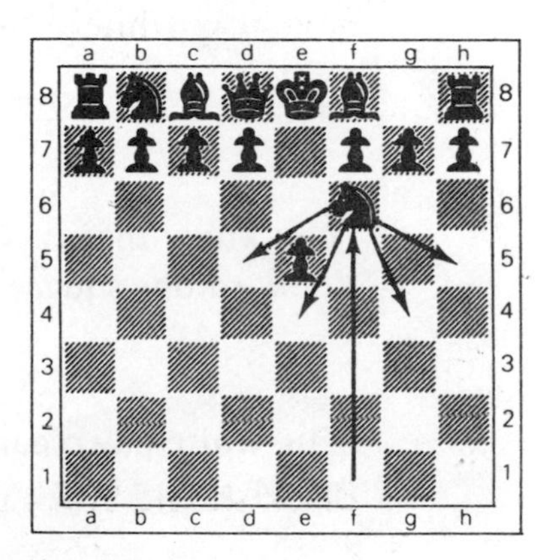

You can try Scholar's Mate for yourself, but it's not a very good idea. You might catch a few people with it, but they won't be good players. If your opponent knows what he is doing he will deal with the threat easily, bringing his pieces into play, and you will just waste time wandering about the board with your queen.

Always be on the look-out for a quick checkmate, always keep a careful watch on f2 and f7, but remember that in the opening your important job is to bring each of your pieces quickly into play on a good square.

En Passant

There is still one more rule of chess you must learn. This is a special pawn capture called **en passant**. You won't meet it very often, which is one reason why we have left it until the very end of the book.

You know that each pawn has a special choice on its first move; it may step forward one square, or it may stride forward two squares.

The white pawn can move forward to d3 or to d4.

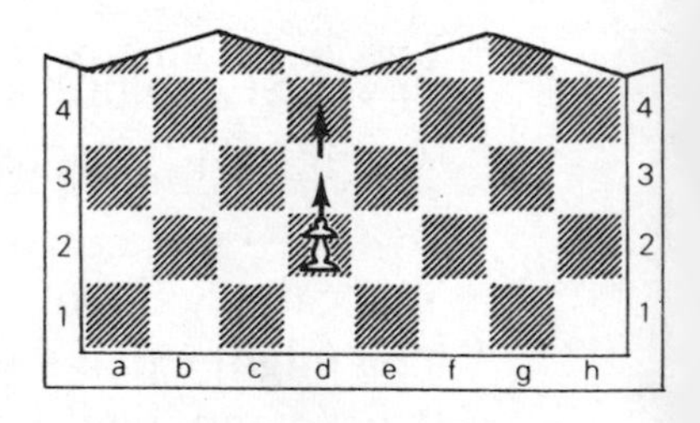

You also know that the pawns attack and capture diagonally forward.
The black pawn attacks b3 and d3.

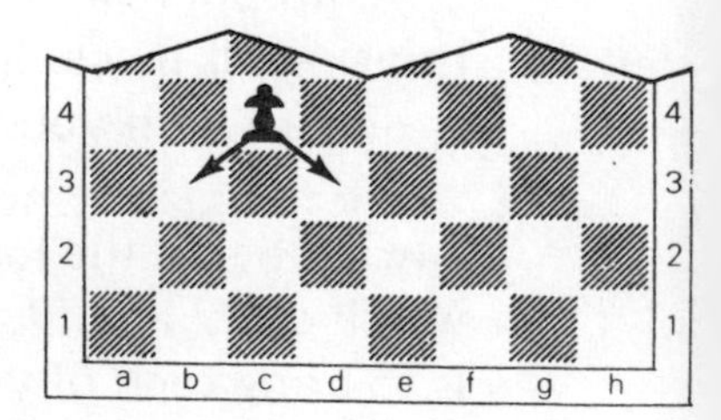

Under the rules as we know them so far, the white pawn could be captured if he moved to d3, but he would be safe if he went to d4.

The *en passant* rule changes this.

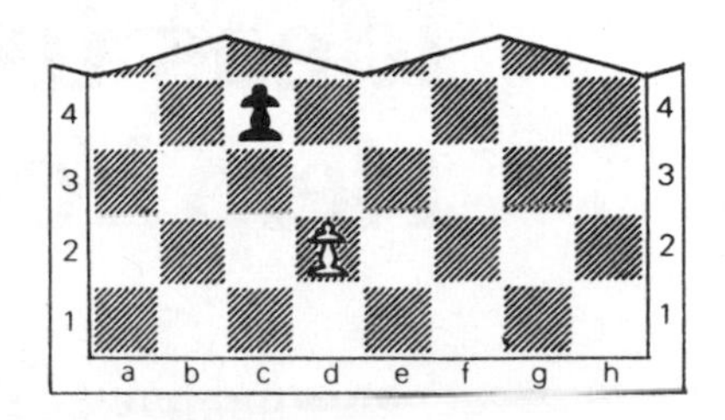

☐ **If a pawn takes advantage of his special choice by moving forward two squares on his first move, then an enemy pawn may capture him as though he had only moved one square.**

So when the white pawn strides forward two squares to d4 . . .

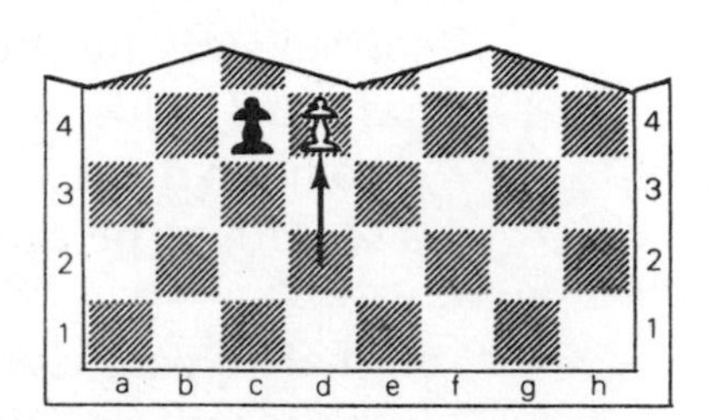

. . . the black pawn may, if he wishes, capture him as though he had only gone to d3.

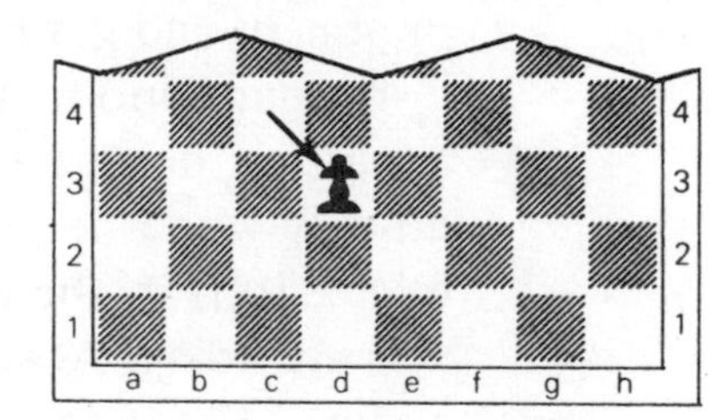

☐ **The *en passant* capture must be made with a pawn.**

☐ **The *en passant* capture must be made the very next move after the pawn has advanced two squares.**

One more example should make the rule absolutely clear.

Black has just moved . . . **c7-c5**.
White cannot play Ne5xc6.
White can play **b5xc6**, but he must do so this move; he cannot wait and capture *en passant* later on.

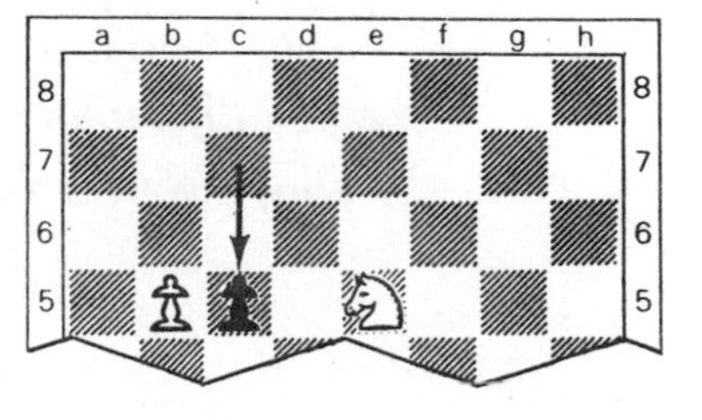

Ideas to Help You Win

You are winning. You are bashing away merrily at your opponent's king . . . you have almost caught him . . . checkmate cannot be far away . . . when . . . crunch! He does something on the other side of the board, something you hadn't seen. Your position collapses, your king is checkmated.

Never forget that there are two of you playing the game; it is easy to get carried away by the excitement of your own attack and forget your opponen has plans of his own. Before moving always ask yourself what your opponent is going to do next. Make sure he isn't threatening anything. Make sure there *is* something he can do next—if there isn't, you've stalemated him!

If after you have moved you see you have made a mistake, don't collapse in a chorus of grunts, groans, and muttered oaths; that will only tell your opponent and get him looking for what you have done wrong.

If your opponent catches you by surprise and you suddenly realize you are losing, don't panic or give up hope and start moving too quickly. Moving quickly won't help you to fight your way out of trouble; thinking hard might. In fact, the best way to avoid making mistakes is to think hard what you are doing. Always take your time; there is never any need to hurry over a move. The longer you think about your position, the longer you take over the move, the more you will see; the less likely you will be to make a mistake; the more likely to find a good move.

Don't make mistakes on purpose! This may sound silly, but you can sometimes set a trap. You play a poor move because you hope your opponent won't see what you are threatening. If your opponent is a weak player he might fall into your trap, if he isn't he will simply take advantage of your mistake, and you will have a rotten position. Always play good moves!

You've now covered your first 23 steps in chess. There are many more ahead of you, but you are well prepared to meet them!

Answers to Quiz Questions

Answers to questions on pages 36 & 37

1. White can give check with his queen: **Qb2-e2+**. White can give check with his f-pawn: **f4-f5+**.

2. Black can move out of check: . . . **Kf6-e6**. Black can block the line of check: . . . **e7-e5**.

3. If Black plays . . . **Qe7-e4**, or . . . **Qe7-b7**, White will be in check. The bad move would be . . . **Qe7-e4+**, because White could then play **Qa4xe4** and win the black queen.

4. No!
White cannot take with his king: **Kc3xd4**, because his king would then be in check from the black pawn on e5.
White cannot take with his e-pawn: **e3xd4**, because his king would then be in check from the black queen on g3.

5. Black can move out of check by: . . . **Kg7-f8**, or . . . **Kg7-g8**, or . . . **Kg7-h7**, or . . . **Kg7-h6**.
Black can escape from the check by capturing the white queen: . . . **Qc5xc3**.
Black can block the line of check by: . . . **f7-f6**, or . . . **Qc5-e5**, or . . . **Qc5-d4**.

Answers to questions on pages 42 & 43

1. White plays **Qd5-a2 mate.**
2. White plays **Qg3-g8 mate.**
3. White plays **Qh3-c8 mate.** (**Qh3-h8+** is not mate because Black can block the line of check with his queen.)
4. White plays **Qe3-e8 mate.**
5. White plays **a7-a8**, the pawn becomes a queen, and the black king is checkmated.
6. White plays **f4-f5 mate.**

Answers to questions on page 65

1. Your board should look like the diagram:
You should have pawns on g6, h5, h3, g2, e2, d3, d5, and e6.

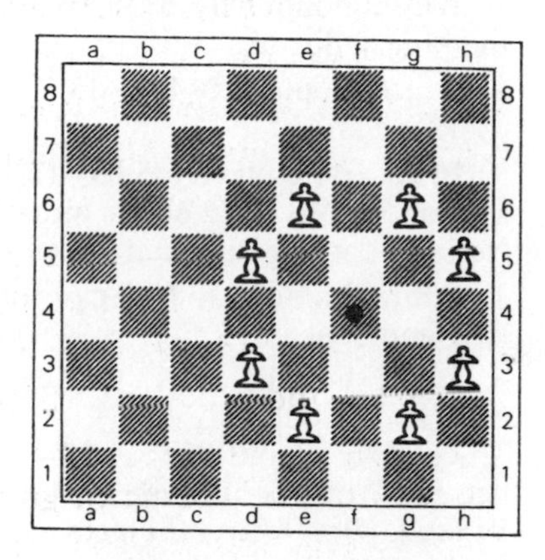

2. The six moves should be:
1 **Nc4xa5**
2 **Na5xc6**
3 **Nc6-e5**
4 **Ne5xg4**
5 **Ng4-f6**
6 **Nf6xh7**

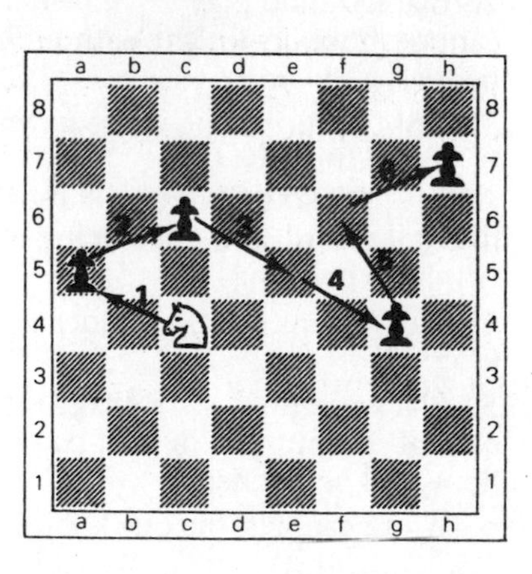

Answers to questions on pages 78 & 79

1. Yes, White can safely play **Nc3-e4**.

2. Black has made a mistake. White will play **Rd1xd4** and if Black recaptures he will lose his queen.

3. Black will lose a pawn: **1 Nc3xd5 e6xd5 2 Bb3xd5**, and if Black captures again he will lose his queen.

Answers to questions on page 83

1. The white rook would attack the bishop and knight from c2 or f5.

2. On f4 the black knight will fork the king and queen.

3. The black bishop will fork the rook and knight from e8 or d3.

Answers to questions on pages 84 & 85

1. White should play **Bf3xc6+** forking the king and rook.

2. White should play **Bb3-d5** forking the rook and knight.

3. Black could play **Nd5-e3+** forking king and rook, but a better move is **Nd5-f4+** forking king and queen.

4. White should play **Ne6-g7+** forking king and queen.

5. Black should play . . . **Qc7-e5** forking rook and bishop.
The bad fork would be . . . **Nb4-c2+** because White could then capture: **Bf5xc2**. (Don't forget! Pieces can move backwards!)

6. White plays **Qe2-e4** and threatens both **Qe4xa8** and **Qe4xh7 mate.**

Answers to questions on pages 89 & 90

1. White should play **Be2-g4** and pin the black queen to her king.

2. Black should play . . . **e5-e4**, and White cannot move his knight without losing his queen.

3. No! Capturing the white pawn would be a dreadful mistake.
After . . . **Qe7xe4** White will move one of his rooks to e1 and the black queen is nailed firmly to her king.

4. **Ra1-a8** pins the black queen to her king.

5. Black can play . . . **Rg8xg3+** and White cannot recapture with his f-pawn because he would be in check.

6. White can win the black knight. After **Nc3xe4** Black cannot play . . . **d5xe4** because of **Qd1xd8 mate.**

Answers to questions on page 91

1. The black king and queen are in line on a diagonal. White can skewer them by **Bg4-f3+**. Black must then move his king, and leave his queen to be captured.

2. White plays **Qd3-h7+** and the black king and rook are skewered.

Answers to questions on pages 96 & 97

1. The white bishop on b2 has a hidden attack on the black king.
White should play **d4-d5+**. Black must then escape from the discovered check, and White will take his rook.

2. White can play **Ne4xf6** and Black will lose his queen if he captures the white knight.

3. Black escapes from check by playing . . . **Bf4-e5+**. Now White is in check from the rook on f8, *and* his queen is threatened.

4. White should play **Bd3xh7+**! Black must get out of check; so he doesn't have time to save his queen.

5. . . . **Rg2xg3** is checkmate.

6. The black rook on e8 and the white king are the important pieces in this position. White should not play **Be2xh5** because Black replies . . . **Be7-b4+** attacking (and pinning) the white queen *and* discovering check.

Answers to questions on pages 102 & 103

1. The white bishop is needed to defend his knight. Black should play . . . **Nd5xe3** and destroy the defender. If White recaptures, he will lose his knight.

2. The black pawn on e5 is pinned to its king; it cannot move and is useless as a defender. White should play **Rf1xf4** winning the knight.

3. The white queen has to defend both rook and knight. Black should play . . . **Rd8xd1+**, and if White retakes he will lose his knight.

4. Black should play . . . **Rd8-d1+**. If the white rook captures he has left his queen undefended; if the white rook doesn't capture, then he will be taken next move.